# THE
# FINANCIAL SECTOR
# OF THE AMERICAN
# ECONOMY

*edited by*
**STUART BRUCHEY**
UNIVERSITY OF MAINE

A GARLAND SERIES

# REPORTING INTEREST RATE SWAPS

## THE ASSOCIATION OF DISCLOSURE QUALITY WITH CREDIT RISK AND OWNERSHIP STRUCTURE

BARBARA TURK ULISS

GARLAND PUBLISHING, INC.
NEW YORK & LONDON / 1994

Library of Congress Cataloging-in-Publication Data

Turk Uliss, Barbara, 1947–
    Reporting interest rate swaps : the association of disclosure quality
with credit risk and ownership structure / Barbara Turk Uliss.
        p.    cm. — (The Financial sector of the American economy)
    Includes bibliographical references and index.
    ISBN 0–8153–1723–9 (alk. paper)
    1. Interest rate futures.   2. Swaps (Finance).    I. Title.  II. Series.
HG6024.5.T87   1994
332.63'23—dc20                                                        93–49429
                                                                              CIP

Printed on acid-free, 250-year-life paper
Manufactured in the United States of America

to Howard and Masen

# Contents

# Acknowledgments

thanks to Gary John Previts,
Robert Colson, Robin Dubin, and Timothy Fogarty

# List of Figures

# Reporting Interest
# Rate Swaps

# Chapter One
# Introduction

During the 1980's, the financial community witnessed the creation of hundreds of types of financial instruments. John Stewart, a partner of Arthur Andersen & Co., and chairman of the American Institute of Certified Public Accountants (AICPA) financial instruments task force, wrote:

> Volatility in interest rates, foreign exchange rates and other prices has created a demand for instruments that could help borrowers, lenders, financial institutions, manufacturers and other industrial companies reduce their risks-risks that if not properly managed could threaten the very survival of their companies. This volatility-combined with increased internationalization, competition, global deregulation, technology, sophisticated analysis techniques and tax and regulatory changes-has promoted an almost unbelievable explosion of innovative financial instruments that may be used as hedging vehicles.

Interest rate swaps were born in the early 1980s and the market has grown to over $1 trillion. The accounting standards say virtually nothing about how either users or market makers should account for these swaps (1989, 48-49).

Financial accounting disclosure of interest rate swaps, (swaps)[1] is the focus of this study. Prior to June, 1990 accounting for swaps was subject only to a requirement under Generally Accepted Accounting Principles (GAAP) for the disclosure of material transactions. More extensive disclosure requirements were established, however, for financial statements issued for fiscal years ending after June 15, 1990 by the provisions of *Statement of Financial Accounting Standards No. 105* (SFAS 105) of the Financial Accounting Standards

Board (FASB) entitled, "Disclosure of Information about Financial Instruments with Off-Balance-Sheet Risk and Financial Instruments with Concentrations of Credit Risk," (FASB 1990).

In this study, pre-SFAS 105 swap disclosures are examined in the context of (1) the quality of disclosure as represented by the number of elements of information either required or proposed by the FASB which are included in the disclosure (2) managers' motives for using swaps, and (3) managers' incentives to disclose swap-related information. The chapter begins with a brief history of the interest rate swap and the environment from which it emerged.

## THE ORIGIN OF THE INTEREST RATE SWAP

Although the most immediate and most often cited impetus for the initial development and increasing use of interest rate swaps is rate volatility, there are several plausible underlying factors which can be interpreted as having fueled their initial popularity and the subsequent development of a market for swaps.

The increase in the volatility of interest rates (as well as exchange rates and prices) which took place in the late 1970s and the 1980s had its roots in world economic events occurring in prior decades. A major example is the demise in the early 1970s of the international payments system established by the Bretton Woods international monetary conference in 1944 (Marshall and Kapner 1990, 3; Brady 1989, 3). Under the Bretton Woods system, the United States had maintained the dollar at fixed rates of exchange with other currencies. After 1971, floating exchange rates were accompanied by increased volatility in interest rates since governments often acted to control exchange rates by manipulating interest rates (Brady 1989).

The direct precursor of the interest rate swap was the currency swap, which in turn is thought to have evolved from the parallel loan. However, while the parallel loan was devised to reduce or avoid the cost of compliance with foreign-exchange regulation, currency and interest rate swaps were developed to manage the risk associated with volatile exchange and interest rates. The first interest rate swap was arranged in London in 1981. Swaps were introduced in the United States when the Student Loan Marketing Association (Sallie Mae) engaged in a "fixed for floating" swap in 1982 (Marshall and Kapner 1990). This timing is not surprising given that in the United States during the 1981-1982 period,

> short-term and long-term interest rates reached record
> levels with a continuation of the extreme volatility in rates
> that began in the fall of 1979...Many corporate treasurers,
> faced with the need to raise funds, went to the short-term
> market rather than attempt to finance at historically high
> and volatile long-term rates. As a result, corporate balance
> sheets became more and more heavily weighted in short-
> term debt. In fact, short-term debt as a percentage of total
> business financing reached an all-time record (Eaker and
> Yawitz 1984, 175).

During the early 1980s swaps were widely touted as an innovative new method of increasing the yields from borrowing. Interest rates could be reduced by borrowing using short-term or revolving agreements and fixing interest rates over a longer term with swaps (Arnold 1984; Ricards 1984). This type of financing was described as attractive for corporations which were looking for fixed, long-term financing but didn't want to incur the cost of issuing long term debt, often because their low credit ratings made such debt too expensive (Arnold 1984; Forsyth 1985). At the same time, a market in swap transactions was being, "created by several large Wall Street firms...ready to make deals on their own accounts around the clock," (Popper 1984, 56).

A change in the competition among bankers seems also to have been related to the proliferation of swaps and other financial instruments. The advent of shelf registration of securities issues (SEC rule 415) in 1982 has been associated with a fundamental change which weakened traditional personal relationships in the investment banking community. Unless an investment banker offered innovative approaches in this newly competitive environment, issuers were likely to hire another banker who could (Kay 1985).

The need to provide innovative financial products also applied to commercial bankers, particularly those in money center banks. The traditional division of duties between them and investment bankers under the Glass-Steagall Act does not prohibit either group from dealing in many of the newly available types of products and services. The provision of interest rate swaps was one of the more profitable service areas in which banks, particularly large money center banks, could compete with investment bankers to expand their own businesses (Weberman 1985). Swaps continued to be used as a marketing tool by bankers throughout the 1980s, even in smaller banks which referred the actual swap business to a money center bank or broker. By initiating a sophisticated transaction such as an interest rate swap for its customer, a small bank might gain the customer's loyalty (Lewis 1989).

Competition between commercial and investment bankers was also heightened by the globalization of financial activity. Since the provisions of Glass-Steagall only apply within the United States, commercial banks increased their efforts to compete on a worldwide basis for financial deals they would not be permitted to participate in within the U.S. Many types of financial instruments were commonly a part of such deals.

> U.S. commercial banks, with far deeper pockets than the average investment bank, can afford to take positions, for example in the currency and interest rate swaps they manage for clients ... if the deal is a winner, the bank makes money from the management fee and also from the profit on the deal itself ... It is the difference between fee income and interest income that chiefly explains why investment banks have enjoyed an average return on equity of 26% over the past five years while commercial banks had to settle for an average 14% return (Weberman 1986, 36).

Another force which fueled the growth of the swaps market in the 1982-1985 period was the economic situation in which thrift institutions found themselves. During the 1981-1982 period of rapidly rising rates, savings and loan institutions holding large portfolios of long-term fixed assets generally suffered losses on their interest-rate spreads. The use of swaps to "fix" rates on their short term liabilities and thereby match incoming cash flows (assets) became a more plausible remedy as the market for swaps grew, allowing swaps to be more easily arranged. In 1985, thrifts were described as, "the main consumers of fixed rate and suppliers of floating," (Ollard 1984, 98) in the interest rate swap markets. Although, through mismanagement and unfortunate planning, some thrift institutions were left with swap-related problems when mortgage interest rates dropped back down (Bartlett 1986) the market for swaps continued to grow.

## INTEREST RATE SWAPS AND DISCLOSURE REGULATION

The burgeoning size of the market for interest rate swaps attracted the attention, not only of current and potential market participants, but also of regulatory bodies, particularly the Bank of England, the Federal Reserve Bank, the Securities Exchange Commission (SEC) and the Financial Accounting Standards Board. Also among those interested in the size of the market were the major participants, or "swap houses," who had a particular interest in assessing their own market shares. Since there is no direct regulation of the market for swaps, its total size has often been reported using figures from "guestimators" who "rely on the intuition of major players in the market," (Shirreff 1985, 251). As recently as 1985, the International Swap Dealers Association's (ISDA),

> sub-committee on market information [was] trying to organize an information pool. Each house would give its volume figures to an independent accountant in full confidence that anonymity would be maintained. Individual market share would then be known only internally, but the global market figure would be public (Shirreff 1985, 251).

The formation of the ISDA, a privately organized, self-regulatory group, was at least partially the result of a realization by major parties that if the swap market,

> doesn't regulate itself, then the regulators may step in and do something inappropriate and extreme.... In October, 1984 two New York City bankers ... were invited to the Fed in Washington to explain the swap market.... The SEC [had] also been talking to the city bankers ... but a meeting in February in Connecticut was perhaps the most important. FASB was host at a round-table discussion for 35 lawyers, bankers and accountants in the swap market ...it was a landmark in drawing market practitioners' attention to the need for self-regulation. ISDA was the obvious forum for further discussion.. [The ISDA was organized despite the fact that their] officers and members

are such a mixed bag of market entities. The investment
and commercial bankers, traditionally bitter enemies, sit
side by side trying to make sense out of a market which has
grown too big for both of them (Shirreff 1985, 253).

The events of the February 5, 1985 meeting of the FASB staff
and major participants in the swaps market were later summarized in
the September, 1985 issue of the *Journal of Accountancy*. Wishon and
Chevalier (1985) wrote:

> The meeting confirmed reports of the spectacular growth
> and increasing popularity of swaps. It also confirmed that
> there has been no comprehensive evaluation of the
> accounting and reporting implications of this new market
> (64).

A citation of their article was still the only "status" reference
listed with regard to the FASB's Emerging Issues Task Force *EITF*
*Abstracts* (Issue No. 84-36), "Interest Rate Swap Transactions," in the
October 6, 1988 edition. As early as 1985, however, the SEC
requested

> that the FASB look into [Financial Instruments related]
> issues and subsequently address them in a major project of
> broad scope (News Report 1986, 14).

In 1986, the FASB added a major project to its agenda to
address issues related to financial instruments and off-balance-sheet
financing. On November 30, 1987 the FASB issued an Exposure Draft
which proposed disclosures regarding financial instruments and
represented the initial phase of the project. This Exposure Draft was
subsequently revised, and the revised draft issued on July 21, 1989. In
March 1990, the FASB issued SFAS 105. Both the Exposure Drafts
and SFAS 105 illustrate the application of disclosure requirements with
a guide to implementation for an interest rate swap. Most recently, in
December, 1990 the FASB issued another Exposure Draft which would
require disclosure of the market value of financial instruments,
including interest rate swaps.

# THE NATURE OF THIS RESEARCH

This study is motivated by works in the accounting literature which deal with issues of accounting disclosure. The basic issues considered arise from the separation of ownership and control in corporations (Berle and Means 1932, Berle 1959) and the function of disclosure in mitigating conflicts between shareholders and managers. Economic incentives for managers to use swaps are examined. It is argued that incentives to use swaps and incentives to disclose information pertinent to their use are associated. It is also argued that managers have incentives to withhold information with regard to swap transactions under circumstances in which that information is important to investors.

# RESEARCH GOALS

This study advances the proposition that information regarding management's intentions with regard to the use of interest rate swaps is important. Management's private information may provide incentives for the use of swaps in circumstances which give rise to potential conflicts between the interests of managers and shareholders. Disclosures of management's intentions and incentives, however, are subject to moral hazard.[2]

The Financial Accounting Standards Board has not required disclosure of managers' reasons for using swaps on the basis that the entity's purpose will often be self-evident based on other required disclosure. In addition, FASB members concluded that

> a requirement to disclose the purpose of entering into certain financial instruments is not necessary because reporting entities are likely to disclose that information to explain more adequately the nature of risks of those instruments, if deemed necessary, (FASB July 1989, paragraph 90; see also FASB March 1990, paragraph 94).

To date, such disclosure is to remain voluntary.

A goal of this project is to identify swap-related issues which have not been considered in the process of developing standards for financial instruments. Since standards for swap-related disclosure will be considered in all phases of the financial instruments project, it is expected that the results of this study will interest agencies deliberating regulatory and disclosure policy.

The study provides a cross-sectional evaluation of interest rate swap disclosures of non-financial firms.[3]  The disclosures studied were included in companies' reports prior to the publication of SFAS 105.[4] These disclosures are evaluated in light of the reporting requirements and recommendations of the FASB in SFAS 105, as well as proposed management incentives for swap use and disclosure.  This study tests the assertions that firms are likely to provide lower quality[5] disclosure when (1) they are relatively greater credit risks, (2) managers exercise considerable discretion over their actions (shareholders' ability to monitor and control are limited) or (3) managerial ownership is low (and the incentives of managers and shareholders are most likely to diverge).

# Notes

1 see Appendix A, Description of an Interest Rate Swap Transaction.

2 Managers may have economic incentives which make it in their own best interest to withhold information.   In addition, their private information is not independently observable and thus is not subject to monitoring.

3 The study will be limited to non-financial firms because financial firms are likely to deal in swap contracts as a revenue-producing activity.   This is likely to dominate incentives for swap usage in financial firms (e.g. savings and loans).

4 The disclosures included were all published after the issuance of the initial Exposure Draft (FASB 1987) and prior to the issuance of the revised Exposure Draft (FASB 1989) in July 1989.

5 An index of disclosure "quality" is developed, based on a set of disclosure attributes. These attributes, based primarily on the suggestions and requirements in SFAS 105, are supplemented by attributes related to managers' incentives for using swaps.

# Chapter Two

# Research Issues and Literature Review

The purpose of this chapter is to present the issue of interest rate swap disclosure as one which merits attention within accounting research. Growth in the use of swaps has made the related accounting disclosure, recognition, and measurement of swap transactions matters of practical interest in the accounting community. Research and experience with similar issues can serve as guides to successful integration of accounting for new financial instruments and business transactions into current GAAP. This study examines the disclosure of swap transactions in the context of current regulatory requirements and of related issues in accounting research.

There are many potential motives for using swaps. Past studies support the view that managers' incentives both for using and for disclosing interest rate swap transactions make information regarding their choices in these areas important to financial information users. *This assumes that managers have both the incentive and the potential to limit disclosure of swaps under certain circumstances.* Manipulation of financial disclosures reduces investors' abilities to assess the value of securities and to monitor managers. As noted by Lev:

> The challenge in this area is to gain insight into the motives and means by which management exercises discretion over financial reporting. Most of the accounting research in this area has been limited to choices *within* GAAP (e.g. the LIFO switch decision.) A systematic examination of managerial choices of non-GAAP procedures is called for. From a normative perspective, this knowledge is relevant to regulators in their efforts to enhance the integrity of capital markets. It will also assist investors and auditors in developing early warning systems to signal manipulation.

Knowledge of managers' motives and means of
manipulation can also be of use in designing contracts with
managers to mitigate manipulation and enhance monitoring
(1989, 185).

The chapter begins with a discussion of current disclosure
requirements for interest rate swaps, related regulatory activity, and
approaches to disclosure regulation suggested in the accounting
literature.  Managers' incentives for using swaps as proposed in the
literature, including both traditional and more recent alternative
explanations, are noted.  One explanation is of particular interest in this
study since it pertains to the type of swap which is most frequently
disclosed by swap users in non-financial firms (Wall and Pringle
1989).   It is the proposition that managers are able to exploit
information asymmetries by choosing to use swaps and short term
borrowing in lieu of long term fixed borrowing (Wall and Pringle
1989; Arak, Estrella, Goodman, and Silver 1988).   Their proposed
motive for a prevalent type of swap use centers on a potential conflict
of interests between managers and shareholders.   That conflict is
discussed in the context of the accounting research literature which
deals with manager/shareholder agency relationships and the separation
of ownership and control.  Managers' incentives to limit or manipulate
swap disclosure, and their potential to benefit by doing so, are
discussed with regard to variations in (1) firm-specific credit risk,  and
(2) the ownership structure of the firm.

## DISCLOSURE REQUIREMENTS FOR INTEREST RATE SWAPS

SFAS 105 (FASB 1990) was the first formal statement to be
issued within the FASB's financial instruments project.[6]   Prior to the
issuance of a formal statement, the FASB (1987) pointed out in their
"Notice for Recipients" in the 1987 exposure draft that financial
instruments had not been adequately reported in firms' financial
statements.  In addition, some companies issued information outside of
their statements which has been characterized as incomplete, not
comparable between firms and even misleading.   In response, the
FASB proposed that requirements for an expanded set of disclosures be
instituted for all financial instruments, including interest rate swaps.

The disclosure requirements established under SFAS 105 apply to all financial instruments with off-balance-sheet risk. The FASB's 1989 exposure draft defines an interest rate swap as an instrument with off-balance-sheet risk, and is consistent with the SFAS 105 definition. SFAS 105 further classifies all interest rate swaps (i.e. those in either a gain or loss position) as having off-balance-sheet market risk (FASB 1989, Appendix B, 22). To date, however, the FASB has not clearly indicated whether interest rate swaps are to be classified as instruments having off-balance-sheet credit risk. Swap disclosures are not addressed individually in either the 1989 exposure draft or in SFAS 105, but an interest rate swap transaction was singled out for use in a model disclosure in both documents. Although it represents a guide for swap disclosure, rather than a required format, the example provided in SFAS 105 is assumed to fulfill the current requirements.

Interest rate swaps (in gain positions) were classified as instruments having off-balance-sheet credit risk as well as market risk in the 1989 exposure draft (FASB 1989, Appendix B, 22). The credit risk classification was dropped in SFAS 105. Also, the scope of the sample swap disclosure in SFAS 105 was reduced by eliminating the quantification of credit risk which had been included in the exposure draft. Despite this, the sample disclosure in SFAS 105 still mentions an exposure, "to credit loss in the event of nonperformance by the other parties to the interest rate swap agreements," (FASB 1990, Appendix C, 26). Since SFAS 105 requires firms to quantify the amount of potential loss for instruments having off-balance sheet credit risk, the status of swaps with regard to credit risk (and related disclosure requirements) is ambiguous based on the FASB's guide to implementation.

SFAS 105 was issued as a result of the first phase of the disclosure portion of the FASB's financial instruments project. It does not provide guidance in some areas which affect swap disclosures such as the specification of appropriate accounting treatments for swaps. For instance, questions of accounting policy like the recognition of income and expense and their timing, and issues of financial instrument valuation have not been addressed. Thomas D'Orazio, an assistant project manager at the FASB, has been quoted as saying,

> The FASB had no intentions of providing anything other than disclosure requirements at this stage... Most of the

reporting difficulty will center around interest rate swaps because there are no authoritative accounting recognition or measurement guidelines (Jarzombek 1989, 47-48).

SFAS 105 does require disclosure of a firm's accounting policy with regard to swaps, since swaps are classified as instruments having off-balance-sheet risk.

Suggestions for swaps-related disclosure have been proposed by many authors including Wishon and Chevalier 1985; Bierman 1987; Riley and Smith 1987; Cummings, Apostolou and Mister 1987; Rue, Tosh and Francis 1988; Stewart 1989; and Nair, Rittenberg and Weygandt 1990. Most proposals emphasize the transfer of risk between swap counterparties and the problems and ambiguities involved in applying existing accounting rules to new financial instruments. The accounting treatment for early termination of a swap contract provides a good example of this. If a swap is characterized as a hedge, *Statement of Financial Accounting Standards No. 80: Accounting for Futures Contracts* (FASB 1987) might be applied in disclosing it, while a swap contract held for speculative purposes might be accounted for more appropriately under Accounting Principles Board (APB) Opinion No. 26 (1972). The FASB's Emerging Issues Task Force Issue No. 874 (FASB 1988) now deals with early swap terminations, providing guidance while the FASB proceeds with the financial instruments project.

Other approaches for swap disclosure have also been proposed. The FASB, in the recognition and measurement phase of the financial instruments project, is considering a fundamental financial instruments approach to resolve questions of accounting for swaps and other instruments. This approach involves viewing each complex financial instrument (e.g. a swap) as being composed of fundamental instruments (e.g. a series of forward contracts). Each fundamental instrument would be subject to specific recognition and measurement (and thus also disclosure) requirements (Bullen, Wilkins, and Woods 1989).

Nair, *et al* (1990) and Bierman (1987) have suggested approaches based on the extensive use of footnotes for swap disclosure. They consider footnotes particularly important for swap disclosure because swaps change the economic position of the firm in ways that aren't captured when journal entries simply record the swap transaction. For example, disclosures including both the swap agreement and the underlying debt may still omit information about changes in the overall matching of firm cash flows attributable to the swap. If the firm's cash inflows are variable and the swap fixes its expected outflows, then a hedge against market fluctuation in interest rates has been removed by the swap. The result is an undisclosed increase in the riskiness of the firm. These authors argue that swap disclosure must go beyond the transaction itself and the related debt, and disclose the relationship of the swap-related obligations to other assets and liabilities of the firm.

## INCENTIVES FOR SWAP USE

Traditional explanations for the use of interest rate swaps are frequently cited in the academic literature. Arbitrage opportunities in credit (e.g. bond) markets are traditionally thought to provide the incentive to swap interest rates. These opportunities arise from firms' abilities to exploit quality spread differentials[7] in available rates for long versus short term debt when companies have different credit risk characteristics (Wall and Pringle 1989; Loeys 1985). Each firm profits from its comparative advantage in credit markets by participating in an interest rate swap and obtaining a lower initial interest rate than it could achieve independently (Bicksler and Chen 1986; Beidleman 1985; Abdullah and Bean 1988; Marshall and Kapner 1990).

It has also been suggested, however, that explanations based on classic arbitrage are not consistent with the rapid growth of the interest rate swaps market (Smith, Smithson and Wakeman 1986, 1988; Arak, *et al* 1988; Wall and Pringle 1989; Loeys 1985; Turnbull 1987; Brown and Smith 1988). Typically, as market participants take advantage of arbitrage opportunities those opportunities are dissipated in competition. It has been noted that as swap use has increased, competition among swap brokers and dealers, as well as market efficiency, have also increased. The associated arbitrage has reduced the potential savings available from using swaps (Marshall and Kapner 1990; Smith 1988; Smith, *et al* 1986). Despite the reduced savings potential, the use of swaps, rather than declining, has become increasingly popular since their initial appearance in 1981. The annual volume (in terms of notional[8] principal) of swaps was estimated to exceed $360 billion by 1987.[9] Figure 1 depicts the estimated total swap contracts outstanding at year-end from 1983 through 1990.[10]

No single cause or benefit has been identified which explains the popularity of swaps. As noted by Cooper and Mello (1991), the issue as to the reason(s) for the use of swaps has been dominant in the academic literature related to swaps. The reduction in interest costs for both parties customarily attributed to a swap is thought to be the principal reason for its use. However, this benefit can be misleading if other differences between the borrowing opportunities aren't considered. For instance, differing maturities, options, or covenants in debt contracts may represent differences in the present value of the combined transactions. This is not taken into account when simply comparing payments under the alternative arrangements (Wall and Pringle 1989; Turnbull 1987; Smith 1988).

## FIGURE 1

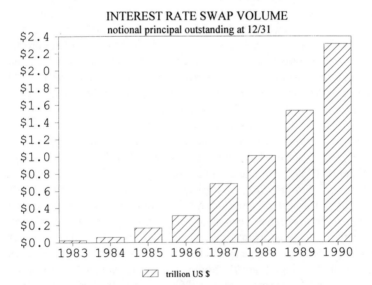

Wall and Pringle (1989) summarize many of the motives for swap use which have been suggested in the literature. They describe the interest rate swaps disclosed during 1986 by firms in the National Automated Accounting Research System (NAARS) database. For example, of 250 swap users, 118 were nonfinancial entities of which 86 were the fixed rate payer. Based on their analysis, they recommend caution in the design of any empirical tests for evidence of a specific motive for swap use. They make this recommendation because their descriptive analysis provides some support for each of several proposed motives but, "no single explanation of swaps is capable of explaining the behavior of all swap users," (Wall and Pringle 1989, 69).

Many explanations which are consistent with the persistent growth in the use of swaps have been suggested. Interest rate swaps have been compared, for instance, to a series of forward (interest rate) contracts (Bullen, *et al* 1989; Smith, *et al* 1986; Brown and Smith 1988). In serving as a replacement for several forward contracts, swaps may, "provide a financial instrument that cannot be duplicated by existing instruments," Turnbull (1987, 16). The availability of swaps would then contribute "to the integration of financial markets by allowing market participants to fill gaps left by missing markets," (Smith, *et al* 1986, 27).[11]

## THE ISSUES OF SWAP DISCLOSURE AND CREDIT RISK

Diversity of the possible motives for using swaps complicates the problem of determining whether swap disclosures provide sufficient information to those who rely on them. Relationships between swaps and other debt are often difficult to assess in published financial statements when they are discernible at all. Also, managers have no obligation to report the available borrowing alternatives which they have not chosen. This makes relationships between current borrowing opportunities and the use of swaps more difficult for financial statement users to detect.

An important characteristic of swaps when viewed from the perspective of disclosure regulation, as suggested by Bierman (1987), Riley and Smith (1987), and Nair, *et al* (1990) is that swaps change the firm's credit risk. Knowledge of swap-related changes in the risk profile of a firm (e.g. in the firm's ability to borrow or to repay debts) is important for investors, but such changes are often not disclosed. A typical description of swaps is best used to illustrate this. Smith, *et al* relate that,

> Trade Journals and market participants agree that the growth of the swaps market has resulted from the ability to

> receive 'significant cost savings' by combining a bond
> issue with a swap. Using swaps, the firm ends up with
> lower borrowing costs than it could have obtained with a
> single transaction. For example, with the use of swaps,
> companies have obtained funding at LIBOR minus 75-100
> basis points (1986, 24).

This description implies that a bond issue (e.g. long term fixed rate debt) can be combined with a swap (trading fixed for floating rate payments) to reduce overall borrowing costs. This type of swap serves to illustrate the potential for undisclosed changes in credit risk of the firm. Participating firms may receive a lump sum (e.g. representing the present value of the incoming fixed rate payment stream) at the inception of the swap, and pay floating rate payments over the remaining life of the agreement.[12] There are many features of this type of arrangement which represent important information for investors. For instance, any overall savings which may result are dependent upon the future movement of interest rates. The initial lump sum payment, computed using an expected series of future interest rates, may not coincide with actual movements in rates over the term of the bond issue. This may result in the amount received being insufficient to allow the firm to cover future payments on the fixed rate debt. The initial cash received represents a resource for satisfying the fixed payment requirements on the original debt, but it must be put to use (invested) over the life of the obligation, and so is effectively additional borrowing. Even when the swap is disclosed, the additional cash outflows (both the fixed and floating rate payments must be made) and the character of the initial increase in cash may not be made clear in a firm's disclosure.

The type of swap described above can also be used by firms to circumvent restrictive covenants in their debt agreements. A firm which is precluded from altering the terms of its debt by refunding it can do so with a swap instead. If interest rates do not change in conformity with expectations at the time of the swap, the firm's ability to repay its debt(s) could decline despite the original lender's protective covenants (Riley and Smith 1987).

Research findings in recent studies cited below relate to the current study in that they represent unexpected changes in the credit riskiness of a firm.[13] The findings provide additional evidence that swap disclosures associated with such changes are important to investors. For example, when managers' private information involves unexpected changes in credit risk[14] related to swaps, shareholders could be harmed despite the fact that many swap disclosures will not affect earnings. In a 1989 study, Burgstahler, Jiambalvo, and Noreen point out the recent interest in investigating the incremental information content of nonearnings information. Their study builds upon research in finance which indicates that changes in the probability of bankruptcy (financial distress) are likely to affect the value of the firm. This effect is attributed to risk aversion on the part of outside parties who deal with the firm (bankers, suppliers, customers, and the like). Their view coincides with that of Shapiro and Titman (1985) who also point out that during periods of financial distress, managers have incentives to make decisions which provide short-term benefits (e.g. decisions to produce inferior goods or reduce safety standards) despite the resulting higher long-term costs. The effects of this type of short-sighted strategy also tend to decrease the value of equity.

Burgstahler, *et al* (1989) use Ohlson's (1980) bankruptcy prediction model to derive a proxy for the probability of bankruptcy, which in turn is used to compute the expected probability of bankruptcy. The difference between the two, representing the unexpected increase (decrease) in the probability of bankruptcy for a given period, is then examined to test for concurrent unexpected decreases (increases) in the value of firm equity.[15] Their results indicate that unexpected changes in the probability of bankruptcy are related to security returns even after controlling for the effect of unexpected earnings.

## MANAGERS' INCENTIVES TO "SWAP TO FIXED"

Most commonly, non-financial firms use interest rate swaps to fix the rates on variable or floating rate borrowings (Wall and Pringle 1989). That particular use of swaps is the focus of papers by Wall 1986, 1989; Loeys 1985; and Arak, *et al* 1988. This "swap to fixed" has also been chosen as the focus of this discussion because it occurs most often and also because it provides an effective illustration of important issues with regard to swap disclosure in the context of accounting research.

Managers may find that fixing interest rates with long term borrowing is advantageous for their firms. They can, however, forego an opportunity to do so and provide the desired fixed rates by substituting a combination of short term borrowings and swaps (Wall 1989; Wall and Pringle 1989; Arak, *et al* 1988). The vulnerability of the borrower to fluctuating interest rates which results from the substitution of short for long term debt is reduced by combining it with a swap. This makes the use of both types of instruments more attractive. For instance, a firm that borrows using a revolving credit agreement with rates that reset frequently can obtain a fixed rate for some intermediate term (e.g. 3-7 years) with a swap. Recent volatility of interest rates has made this use of swaps more popular (Turnbull 1987). As the demand for swaps, and the availability of market-makers (financial institutions acting as swap intermediaries) have grown, transaction costs associated with swaps have been reduced (Whittaker 1987) also making them more attractive. In addition, swaps are better suited for use in fixing interest rates than potential substitutes, such as futures contracts, since they are available for longer maturities and under more flexible terms (Turnbull 1987).

Swap-related debt is generally associated with variable rates and shorter terms than the borrowing alternatives foregone by managers. As Loeys (1985, 23-24 and note 11) reports:

> the quality spread that is typically quoted does not refer to debt of the same maturity. The floating-rate debt that firms use as a basis for swaps is mostly short to medium-term, while the fixed-rate debt consists of long-term bonds... The floating rate debt that firms use as a basis for a floating-to-fixed interest rate swap consists mostly of bank credit, commercial paper, certificates of deposits (CDs), and floating-rate notes (FRNs). More than 90% of commercial and industrial loans by U.S. banks are short term. Commercial paper usually has a maturity of 3 to 6 months, while most large negotiable CDs of financial institutions are for 6 months or less. Although FRNs have stated maturities of 7 to 15 years, almost all FRNs issued in the U.S. have covenants that give the holder the right to redeem the note at 3-year intervals.

Long term funding carries a higher interest rate because a risk premium to the lender is included in its cost. Part of that premium covers the long term lender's cost of bearing the risk that the borrower's ability to repay the debt will deteriorate in future periods. While the risk premium is "saved" by the short term borrower in the current period, the underlying risk that the firm will become a less attractive candidate for credit in future periods must be assumed by the firm's shareholders and its managers (Loeys 1985).

Management's private information about the firm's future credit standing may differ from that available to lenders in the credit markets. When such a difference occurs, a conflict of interests can arise between shareholders and managers, resulting in the possibility that shareholders can be harmed by managers who act out of self-interest. For example, consider the incentives of managers who have the current options of (1) engaging in long term fixed-rate borrowing or (2) using short term borrowing which must be renegotiated each period in combination with a swap. Managers who are privately aware that circumstances affecting the firm would make it difficult to contract for comparable debt in future periods[16], might still choose to borrow short term funds and engage in a swap currently. When they believe that the market's assessment of the firm's future credit standing is overly optimistic (and thus long term debt is "underpriced" for their firm) then in choosing the short term and swap alternative they will *fail to maximize firm value*. (That is, the firm's value would be higher if the managers took advantage of lenders' beliefs and locked in "underpriced" long-term financing). Managers' personal benefits from acting in their own interest might include higher current bonuses or reputations temporarily enhanced by higher current reported earnings or healthier looking cash positions. If costs are incurred by the firm in future periods because its managers did not secure long term financing at favorable rates, this cost is likely to be borne, at least in part, by the firm's shareholders.

Managers' incentives to engage in self-interested behavior to the detriment of shareholders will increase with their firm-specific human capital.[17] In situations of financial distress it is likely that managers with an investment in firm-specific human capital have more at risk than shareholders who can diversify their holdings in the capital market, and so their incentives to engage in opportunistic[18] behavior are increased (Shapiro and Titman 1985). They are likely to be more willing than fully informed shareholders would be to take risks currently, relying upon their personal abilities to overcome anticipated adversity in future periods.

These arguments assume that it is possible for managers to act opportunistically and benefit from the use of private information. This is in keeping with the perspective on accounting method choice which assumes self-interested behavior on the part of managers. Holthausen, notes,

> Unless one is willing to assume that a manager's human capital declines by the amount of any loss in firm value which results from the opportunistic choice of accounting methods as opposed to the most efficient choice of accounting methods (such that *firm value* is maximized), a self-interest theory of accounting choice need not lead to the same predictions about the selected set of procedures as the efficiency perspective[19] (1990, 208). (emphasis supplied)

Managers' incentives to choose a combination of short term debt and swaps despite the failure of that choice to maximize firm value also have implications for accounting disclosure of swaps. When managers have private information with regard to probable revisions in the firm's credit standing, their expectations are not realized until future periods. That information would be revealed in subsequent periods only given a portion of the set of possible outcomes. For instance, given their private information, managers may estimate there is a 75% probability that credit risk will deteriorate when potential creditors (the "market") would set the probability at 50%. If the potential adverse circumstances anticipated by managers (which prompted this difference in expectations) don't materialize, the other contracting parties may never discover that they were at risk. More importantly, if managers' expectations are realized, and losses are inflicted on parties to the firm, there is no compelling reason to assume that managers' prior expectations will become apparent.

In the case of the "swap to fixed", opportunistic behavior of managers has two components, (1) choosing short term debt and a swap when contracting for long-term fixed debt is in the best interests of the firm and its owners and (2) either failing to disclose the swap or disclosing insufficient information for the implications of their choice to be discerned by outside parties. Managers who enjoy the benefits of these actions in the form of enhanced current reported results have an incentive to avoid full disclosure of swaps and related transactions in order to protect their private information.[20] This assumes, of course, that managers are able to benefit from the use of private information. That is an assumption which continues to be debated in the literature.

## AGENCY RELATIONSHIPS IN THE ACCOUNTING LITERATURE

The cost of managerial failure to maximize firm value is associated with the relationship between owners and managers and the separation of ownership and control. It is generally known as an agency cost. The potential for managers to impose agency costs on shareholders supports the argument that disclosures are important to shareholders in their task of monitoring management.

An agency relationship is one in which one party, the principal, contracts with another party, the agent, to engage in an activity on behalf of the principal. This may entail delegation to the agent of decision-making authority on behalf of the principal. An agency relationship between two self-interested individuals (principal and agent) will give rise to a conflict of interests between the parties when the incentives of the parties diverge (Jensen and Meckling 1976; Jensen and Smith 1984). Costs incurred by parties to the agency relationship in either monitoring the activities of the other party, or providing assurance that the interests of the parties are aligned are agency costs. Agency costs also generally include the costs of contracting, and the costs identified by Jensen and Meckling (1976) as the residual loss. The residual loss represents the opportunity cost of actions which may not be optimal but are taken because it is not cost effective to enforce contracts perfectly. At the time contracts are negotiated, the parties anticipate the incentives of other parties to the contract and the costs of their expected actions are reflected in the contract terms. That is, each party attempts to "price protect" itself against expected costs of harm from other parties. Some party, "can always benefit by devising more effective ways of reducing" these agency costs (Jensen and Smith 1984, 7).

A literature based on the framework of contracting or "positive agency"[21] has developed in both finance and accounting. As noted by Jensen and Smith (1985),

> The substantial attention devoted to developing a theory of agency has resulted in two approaches, which we refer to as the 'positive theory of agency' and the 'principal-agent'

literatures. Although they differ in many respects, both literatures address the contracting problem among self-interested individuals and assume that in any contracting relationship total agency costs are minimized....The principal-agent literature has concentrated more on analysis of the effects of preferences and asymmetric information and less on the effects of the technology of contracting and control (96).

The positive agency literature, adopts the efficient markets hypothesis[22] as well as rational expectations in debt markets (Watts and Zimmerman 1986). It assumes that expected costs of agency relationships between managers and either shareholders or bondholders will be provided for in the contracting process and borne by managers. Fama (1980) also argues that agency costs are borne by managers when ownership and control are separated. He asserts that managers must face "ex post settling up" in the managerial labor market for agency costs inflicted on other parties to the contract. That is, they have economic incentives to minimize agency costs because they invariably bear those costs themselves.

## THE ISSUE OF PRICE-PROTECTION

While the arguments presented in this study generally rest on the positive agency literature, one of the basic assumptions of that literature is not adopted in this study. This is the assumption of price protection among the contracting parties, particularly the associated assumption of their  inability to profit from the use of private information.  The price protection assumption has its origin in the combined ideas of natural selection in the survival of organizations (Fama and Jensen 1983a; Watts and Zimmerman 1986), and the characterization of the firm as a nexus of contracts between agents (Jensen and Meckling 1976). It also rests on the premise that parties to contracts (including managers) have incentives to make accounting choices which minimize agency costs for all parties concerned, and that this results in maximizing firm value. Holthausen (1990) refers to this as the efficiency perspective. From the efficiency perspective, when any of the contracting parties can be anticipated to act out of self interest in a manner which harms other parties, the others will protect themselves by pricing contracts to prevent being harmed. Activities in prior periods will be observed and incorporated into these expectations. Parties who take advantage of others will not survive over time as participants in the market of contracting parties.

In studies dealing with situations in which there is a separation of ownership and control, it is sometimes assumed that managers' interests will be aligned with those of shareholders (e.g. Fama 1980). This is consistent with the notions of price protection and the inability to profit from private information but, empirically, is not compelling. Justification for securities legislation and regulation of financial reporting in the United States is based on the expectation of problems due to a conflict of interests between these two groups and the associated potential effects on corporate disclosure (Berle and Means 1932; Beaver 1981, 11-15). Regulators are likely to claim that disclosure rules exist primarily to protect shareholders and other users of financial information.

The principal-agent literature mentioned above incorporates the potential for information asymmetries in capital markets. Findings of information content in numerous studies of securities market reactions to releases of financial disclosures (e.g. earnings announcements)[23] serve to confirm that those disclosures have information content. Much of the empirical literature beginning with Ball and Brown (1968) has been designed to test the efficiency of the capital markets. These studies tend generally to support market efficiency but also to cast doubt on a strict interpretation of price protection which is based on the assumption of costless availability of information. Ball reports,

> it is clear from Ball and Brown (1968) that there are gains
> from obtaining private information on earnings before 'the
> market' does--that is, before it becomes publicly-available
> (1990, 11).

It follows that those gains come at the expense of other interested parties in "the market" who had no access to that information. When the efficiency perspective is replaced with the possibility that managers can retain private information and benefit from having done so, it is no longer clear that shareholders and creditors are price-protected. The question of which parties bear agency costs then becomes an *empirical* one. The potential for managers to benefit from the use of private information without invariably being subject to the discipline of price protection (or ex-post settling up) cannot be ruled out.

## WALL'S AGENCY EXPLANATION: CREDITORS VS OWNER-MANAGERS[24]

Wall (1986, 1989) provides an explanation for the use of swaps which is based on agency theory and also consistent with the continuing growth of the swaps market. It is also based on the use of short term debt and swaps in lieu of long term debt to reduce agency costs. He points out that this use of swaps reduces conflicts between the interests of owner-managers and creditors.

Short term borrowing limits owner-managers' economic incentives to take agency-cost related actions which benefit themselves at the expense of creditors. For instance, owner-managers have economic incentives to invest in projects which are sufficiently risky to cause the overall level of the firm's risk of default to increase. This type of investment effectively transfers value away from bondholders by increasing the level of risk they must bear on a fixed return, and thereby reduces the value of their claims on the firm. Owner-managers, as the firm's residual claimants, can expect to enjoy any increase in payoffs produced by the riskier strategy if it succeeds, without increasing their own downside risk if the firm fails. In particular, if the firm is in financial distress its residual claimants are already likely to receive nothing if a risky "last ditch" project fails and the firm enters bankruptcy.

Alternatively, owner-managers have incentives to underinvest in projects which they consider suboptimal from a net present value perspective (i.e. projects which are not risky enough to provide a high return) but would improve interest coverage for bondholders. This means owners will avoid taking actions which would concurrently reduce the bondholders' risk of carrying the debt and increase the current value of the contractually fixed return on their bonds.

Wall (1989) argues that a portion of the premium on long term debt is included by creditors to protect themselves from this type of activity. Since short term credit contracts are renegotiated frequently, owner-managers are limited in their ability to impose the agency costs described above on creditors. They are also less likely to try, since creditors will simply adjust the terms they offer in the upcoming period to the current risk profile of the borrower. The reduction in agency costs provides Wall's explanation for the growth in the use of swaps, coupled with the use of short term debt when debt markets are competitive.

Wall's approach differs from that of the current study because it addresses only the owner-manager/creditor relationship. It provides an alternative explanation for use of a "swap to fixed" since costs attributable to that particular agency relationship are saved, and not just shifted to another party. Also, as noted by Wall and Pringle (1989), the riskier the firm the greater the savings.

Wall's explanation of swap use is not likely to explain variation in swap disclosure, however. Since this type of cost reduction is "good news" for shareholders, managers would have no apparent incentive to withhold the information. In firms which are not entirely owner controlled, swap-related arguments with regard to managers' incentives and private knowledge of upcoming changes in firm credit risk still apply.

## OWNERSHIP STRUCTURE: IN CONTEXT

In this study, the traditional characterization of corporate ownership is assumed. That is, agency relationships between owners and creditors are expected in any firm which is not completely owner financed, and between these two parties and managers when a firm is not entirely owner managed. It is important to note, however that the lines of the agency relationship between managers and non-controlling shareholders which was the concern of Berle and Means (1932) have become blurred in recent years. The rise of new classes of intermediaries who serve as defacto agents for shareholders separates even further the elements of ownership and control (*The Economist* 1990, 1991). These new arrangements can be broadly classified into two major groups, those which have been established by way of corporate reorganizations such as leveraged buyouts, and those which have resulted from the proliferation of institutionalized investing through pension plans, direct investment in mutual funds, and the like.

Arguments have been made that control over managers is being accomplished by way of corporate reorganizations, and in particular, leveraged buyouts. Firmer control results both from the ownership of instruments which combine equity and debt of the newly reorganized entities, and the greater discipline imposed upon managers by the high levels of debt carried by these companies. This is the perspective of Jensen (1986, 1989). He argues that managers in industries which are in low-growth, cash rich, or declining sectors have incentives to cause their firms to grow beyond their optimal size. Firms in these sectors will therefore reorganize to effectively eliminate this problem by creating a group of active investors,

> who hold large equity or debt positions, sit on boards of directors, monitor and sometimes dismiss management, are involved with the long-term strategic direction of the companies they invest in, and sometimes manage the companies themselves (Jensen 1989, 65).

The other major type of relationship inserted between shareholders and managers is that of institutional investors (e.g. professional fund [portfolio] managers). Again there are two major lines of argument as to the effect of this on the question of owner/manager corporate control.

It has been argued (*The Economist* 1990) that institutional investors are simply "punter capitalists" who have forsaken the role of proprietor and the notion of stewardship. It is assumed that their primary interest is portfolio growth and that at the first sign of trouble for a firm in their investment portfolio they promptly sell their shares. Therefore, they are expected to "vote with their feet" rather than attempt to exercise active control over management to protect ownership interests and promote long-term growth.

In contrast, some institutional investors have shown more of an interest in investing for the long term in certain corporations and then exercising control over managers in those firms on the strength of their large ownership stakes (Wayne 1990). Jensen (1989) and Light (1989) cite the increasing frequency with which institutions have taken large equity positions in firms in the form of private placements. This allows fund managers to exercise active control over a smaller number of investments, and rely less on the mechanics of portfolio management in generating target returns.

# OWNERSHIP STRUCTURE:
# THE RESEARCH FOCUS

In earlier sections of this chapter it was argued that motives for the most common use of swaps are associated with a conflict of interests between owners[25] and managers of firms. This conflict arises out of managers' ability to benefit by engaging in swap transactions which are in their own best interests (e.g. reported results look better, current cash flows are increased, borrowing is made possible) but not necessarily in the best interests of the firm and its owners. Managers' ability to benefit is in part dependent on their ability to protect private information about their motives and activities. This in turn, will be reflected in the quality of swap disclosures. Issues involving the separation of corporate ownership and control, and attendant conflicts between owners and managers, have served to motivate many studies in accounting research. This section provides the argument for an association between the quality of swap disclosures and the ownership structure of firms.

Swap disclosures and ownership structure are likely to be related, based on the hypothesis of Dhaliwal, Salamon and Smith who argue,

> that the accounting methods adopted by a firm are influenced by whether a firm is management or owner controlled. Specifically this line of argument leads to the prediction that management controlled firms are more likely than owner controlled firms to adopt accounting methods which result in increased or early reported earnings (1982, 52).

The application of their hypothesis in the context of interest rate swap usage may appear unorthodox since the use of swaps does not constitute a choice between accounting methods. In the firms to be studied, however, the use of swaps represents management's choice between two methods of fixing the interest rate on a portion of the firm's debt.[26] The outcome of this choice affects the amount of reported interest expense, and thus reported income, for these firms. This is the case even if it is expected (by all parties) that the net present values of the two alternatives at the time the choice is made are the same, assuming competitive markets (Turnbull 1987).[27] Also, the magnitude of the effect of this choice on reported earnings will be positively related to the level of credit risk of the firm. Managers of firms with lower credit ratings will generate larger apparent "savings" of credit risk premiums by choosing a short term debt and swap combination over long term debt. Managers thus have a greater incentive to choose this type of financing arrangement as the firm's credit standing becomes less favorable.

Dhaliwal, *et al* support their hypothesis in part by citing Williamson's (1967) earlier hypothesis that:

> managers of management-controlled (MC) firms exercise control over the information released regarding firm performance in an attempt to present the results of firm operations in a most favorable way. The attempt to control information is intended to keep current shareholders satisfied and unwilling to support any takeover attempts by outside groups. This line of argument suggests that the managers of MC firms are likely to choose accounting methods which result in higher or early reported earnings and higher reported equity. (1982, 43)

In addition, they cite the assumption that management compensation is associated with company profits. The argument is further developed by pointing out that Zmijewski and Hagerman (1981) following Watts and Zimmerman (1978) base their work,

> on the two propositions that (1) managers attempt to maximize their utility, and (2) that their utility is positively related to their compensation. The notion that management utility is tied to the amount and timing of compensation leads to the hypothesis that MC firms will be more inclined than owner-controlled (OC) firms to choose accounting methods which result in higher or earlier reported income, (Dhaliwal, *et al* 1982, 44).

Although they cite many earlier works which provide arguments and evidence that, "there may be a systematic difference in the accounting methods adopted by MC and OC firms," (1982, 45), Dhaliwal, *et al* provide the earliest direct test of the hypothesis that MC firms are more likely to choose income or equity increasing accounting methods than OC firms. Their results supported this hypothesis.[28]

When ownership and control are separated, alternative mechanisms have been used to motivate managers to resolve conflicts in favor of shareholders. The use of audits to monitor financial disclosures is a important example (Jensen and Meckling 1976). An audit tests management's assertion that financial reporting is in conformity with GAAP.

Generally accepted accounting principles, even after the provisions of SFAS 105 are instituted, require only limited disclosure of material swap transactions,[29] with much detail (e.g. the relationship(s) of a swap with assets or liabilities) disclosed at management's discretion. An audit is not likely to provide comprehensive monitoring of items which are beyond the scope of GAAP. Because initial requirements for swap disclosures do not apply to fiscal years ending before June 1990,[30] the ability of non-managers to monitor swap-related activity during the period covered by this study was limited. Since a potential conflict of interest between managers and owners exists, and that conflict will be characterized by information asymmetries between the parties, management's disclosures are subject to moral hazard (see Note 2, Chapter 1).

Three recent papers which examine the ownership structure issue rest upon Dhaliwal, Salamon and Smith's general hypothesis. Building on the empirical work of Morck, Shleifer and Vishny (1988), Francis and Wilson (1988) and Niehaus (1989) also address this issue. In all of these later studies, the level of managerial ownership[31] is examined in the context of an conflict of interests between owners and managers. An independent variable represents management ownership in each study. This facilitates testing for a relationship between the dependent variable in each study,[32] and the level of management ownership.

All three studies test for an expected non-linear relationship between management ownership and the dependent variable based on two conflicting hypotheses. The first is that at low levels of managerial ownership, the interests of owners and managers vary most widely. Their interests are then assumed to converge (or become aligned) as the level of management ownership grows and as managers' positions as owners increase (Jensen and Meckling 1976). Both Francis and Wilson (1988) and Morck, *et al* (1988) refer to this as the *convergence-of-*

*interests hypothesis*, while Niehaus (1989) uses the term *incentive alignment* to represent this convergence.[33]

The second hypothesis holds that management's actions and ability to act out of self-interest are constrained by owners' abilities to effectively monitor managers. For instance, assume that managers have incentives to combine short term debt with swaps in order to increase current reported earnings when this is not in the best interests of shareholders. A manager's ability to benefit from this type of action is curtailed when shareholders effectively monitor the managers' activities and penalize opportunistic behavior. Major impediments to shareholders' monitoring and control efforts are likely to exist when:

> (1)     ownership is diffuse, (the number of shareholders is very large) making it more costly and difficult for owners to organize for purposes of monitoring and disciplining management (Alchian and Demsetz 1972; Francis and Wilson 1988; Schipper 1981) and, the incentive to monitor is reduced because risk-bearing is spread over a large group of shareholders (residual claimants) who may also diversify across organizations.

> (2)     management holds an ownership stake which is large enough to allow them to effectively control the company's affairs without being subject to shareholder discipline, that is, management is entrenched and relatively impervious to the demands of shareholders (Demsetz 1983; Fama and Jensen 1983a, 1983b; Francis and Wilson 1988; Morck, *et al* 1988; Berle 1959).

The opposing effects of the convergence of interests and the fluctuating strength of management's discretion (or entrenchment)[34] in the face of shareholder discipline make it very difficult to predict the relationship between the level of managerial ownership in a firm and the ability of its managers to impose agency costs on shareholders.[35]

The descriptive study of Morck, *et al* (1988) provided evidence of a non-linear relationship between firm value and managerial ownership. Their results were interpreted as an indication that the convergence of interests effect was dominant when management ownership was between 0 and 5%, and over 25%, while the entrenchment effect (resulting in a drop in firm value) was dominant[36] between approximately the 5% and 25% management ownership levels (Morck, *et al* 1988, Fig. 1, 301).

Francis and Wilson (1988) included separate independent variables to test hypotheses relating to diffusion of ownership and managerial ownership. Their reported results were not significant with regard to managerial ownership. The variable they used to represent diffusion of ownership was very similar to that used by Dhaliwal, *et al* (1982) to identify OC firms. They created a dichotomous variable which was "coded one if the largest individual owner has ten percent or more of outstanding stock," (Francis and Wilson 1988, 667) and zero otherwise. In their test of this variable, they hypothesize that, "firms with more diffuse ownership are more likely to use a higher-quality auditor" (1988, 667). This hypothesis is based on the assumption of Francis and Wilson (1988) that a firm with diffuse ownership (MC) will be more likely to have a higher-quality audit as a part of its control system since monitoring is more difficult when ownership is diffuse. Their reported results classify this variable as "weakly significant" (t=1.06 and 1.03 in their probit and OLS models respectively), but having positive rather than the expected negative signs for these coefficients. This reversal of the signs from the result which had been expected by Francis and Wilson (1988) is consistent with the interpretation of Dhaliwal, *et al* (1982), however, who expect firms with greater diffusion of ownership[37] (MC firms) to be under less restrictive control than firms in which ownership is more concentrated. That is, in keeping with Dhaliwal, *et al* (1982), Francis and Wilson (1988) could have included as an alternative hypothesis: greater diffusion of ownership will result in greater managerial discretion and less restrictive control, including a lower quality audit. That alternative hypothesis is consistent with the results of the Francis and Wilson study and also with the arguments described at length above.

In his 1989 study, Niehaus tests for the probability that a firm's managers will choose LIFO over FIFO when there are cross-sectional differences in ownership structures. It is assumed that owners prefer LIFO since it is the tax-minimizing method, while managers prefer FIFO, the income-maximizing method. Given these preferences and the associated conflict of interests between managers and owners, Niehaus (1989) expects that when the level of management ownership is high, managers have greater discretion and will act in their own interest (e.g. choose FIFO). He also cites the opposing expectation that as ownership increases, managers' incentives will be aligned with those of owners, making them more likely to choose LIFO. Niehaus (1989) constructs his model based on the expectation that when combined, "these two hypotheses can lead to a non-monotonic relation between managerial ownership and the inventory method choice" (283). The results and their interpretation in the Niehaus (1989) study were generally consistent with those of Morck, *et al* (1988)[38]. That is, as managerial ownership increased, the probability of choosing LIFO initially decreased, but then reached a point beyond which it increased. This result was interpreted as dominance of (1) managerial discretion over lower levels of managerial ownership, and (2) the convergence of interests, or alignment effect, at higher levels. In both this and the Morck, *et al* (1988) study, this reversal occurred at approximately the 25% level of ownership.

The research approach in this study with regard to ownership structure is based on the general assumption that when managers' incentives conflict with those of owners, managers will be more likely to take action favorable to their own interests if; (1) they have greater discretion (freedom from shareholder monitoring and control) over their actions and (2) their level of ownership is low. Accordingly, the quality of disclosure of interest rate swap transactions is expected to vary with regard to ownership level in a non-linear fashion. That is, the quality of disclosure is expected to be lower when the entrenchment effect is strongest and higher when the alignment effect is dominant.

## SUMMARY

Several series of related studies in accounting research have been cited to provide evidence in support of the arguments that (1) the disclosure of interest rate swaps is an important source of information for investors and (2) managers have incentives to limit their disclosure under certain circumstances. The extent and form of swap disclosure which is needed to convey the information required by investors is currently being debated in the accounting literature and by regulatory authorities. Information about the quality of disclosure based on current and recently proposed requirements will provide insight as to systematic variations in the swap disclosure provided by firms. Related implications can then be considered in the regulatory process.

Research supports the predictions that the availability of swap-related information, as reflected in the quality of swap disclosure, will be related to both the credit risk profile and ownership structure of a firm. That relationship is based on management's incentives with regard to both the use of swaps and the disclosure of related information. It is argued that in the case of swaps used to fix short term debt, managers are likely to have incentives and the ability both to use swaps and to limit disclosure of those swap transactions. The arguments are based on a self-interest theory of accounting choice and a managerial motive for using swaps in a manner which conflicts with the interests of shareholders.

The arguments lead to the prediction that managers' incentives to use swaps increase as firm credit risk rises. That is because as firms have more difficulty in obtaining credit from lenders, the risk premiums they must pay for long-term borrowing increase. Reducing the payment of risk premiums by choosing instead to combine short-term debt and swaps then becomes increasingly lucrative.

The arguments presented also support (1) the assertion that managers have incentives to limit swap disclosure and (2) the prediction that the likelihood of their doing so increases with managerial discretion and decreases with the level of their ownership in the firm.

The research hypotheses derived from these predictions, and the methods to be employed in testing them are described in Chapter 3.

# Notes

6 On December 31, 1990, the FASB issued an Exposure Draft (FASB 1990) which, if it results in a formal pronouncement, would require disclosure of the market value of many financial instruments, including interest rate swaps. None of the disclosures examined for this dissertation included the market value of swaps.

[7] The quality spread is the difference between rates for firms of different risk levels on debt of the same denomination and maturity, while the "quality spread differential" is the difference between quality spreads at two different maturities, long and short (Wall and Pringle 1989, 60).

[8] The "notional principal" amount is the dollar amount on which interest calculations for swap payments are based. Typically, this amount is notional in that it does not represent any exchange of principal, but rather is simply used as a base figure in computing interest.

[9] Market surveys of annual volume of swaps have been conducted for the International Swap Dealers Association. The lack of regulation of swaps evidently precludes an accurate accounting as published estimates vary widely (Wishon and Chevalier 1985, 3). For instance, Brown and Smith (1988, 51) cite an estimated $900 billion in notional principal by the end of 1987.

[10] 1983-4 (Ricards 1984), 1985-86 (ISDA 1987), 1987-1990 (ISDA 1991).

[11] This explanation is also consistent with the management incentives to use swaps with regard to underlying debt which are discussed in this study.

[12] See the 1988 Annual Report of NALCO Chemical Company or Scott Paper Company, for example.

[13] The concepts of a firm's probability of bankruptcy and its level of credit riskiness are synonymous, with the caveat that the former concept might be interpreted as the more extreme.

[14] Note that in the case of swaps such changes would be unexpected from the point of view of the market, but would be "privately expected" by managers.

[15] The authors argue that, "financial information actually affects the set of production and investment opportunities which face the firm - thus directly affecting the value of equity. In particular, ... that information related to solvency affects the value of equity through its effect on the implicit contracts entered into with stakeholders." They acknowledge, however that results of their study could also be interpreted as an indication that, "unexpected changes in the probability of bankruptcy convey information incremental to earnings by surrogating for unspecified 'good news/bad news'" (223).

[16] For example they have become aware that a hidden defect may exist in their major product line. This discovery would make a financially debilitating recall necessary in the following period.

[17] Firm-specific human capital includes non-transferable knowledge of the firm's systems and production processes, personal working relationships with others within the firm, and the like.

[18] In this study, managers' opportunistic behavior is defined as managers' actions which are in their own self-interest, but counter to the best interests of related parties, particularly shareholders or creditors.

[19] The efficiency perspective is described in greater detail later in this chapter.

[20] Shareholders with full information regarding the nature and effect of the related transactions will revise their expected values of their holdings in the firm (or the amount they will be willing to pay for equity shares) accordingly. A swap disclosure which has information content with regard to managements' expectations regarding credit risk volatility would serve as a signal to statement users (market participants), resulting in an adjustment in security prices.

[21] The literature cited here is also often referred to as synonymous with or closely related to the property rights or contracting literature or the theory of the firm (see Jensen and Meckling 1976; Smith 1776; Coase 1937; Alchian and Demsetz 1972; Watts and Zimmerman 1986, 179-199).

[22] This includes the general assumption that "competition for information drives the expected economic profits from the production and use of information to zero" (Watts and Zimmerman 1986, 35).

23 Security price reactions indicating information content in earnings announcements such as those in Ball and Brown (1968) have been documented empirically with much more success (i.e. with statistically significant findings) than those studies which test for similar effects of accounting changes (Foster 1986).

24 Wall's arguments focus on the agency relationship between the owners (including their agents) of a firm and its creditors. The term owner-manager is used for clarity to emphasize the distinction between that particular agency relationship and the relationship between owners and managers.

25 The term owner used in this sense generally refers to the legal owner of shares, but as noted earlier the claims of legal owners are often subject to the actions of intermediaries such as fund (portfolio) managers who operate in a fiduciary capacity.

26 It is possible that the disclosure of the relationship between a swap and a portion of the firm's debt will enable non-managers who have knowledge of debt markets to assess the opportunity costs of management's actions, and for shareholders to be made aware of the risks that may have been shifted to them.

27 As reiterated by Wall and Pringle (1989, 60), Turnbull (1987) "shows that interest rate swaps are a zero-sum game in the absence of market imperfections and swap externalities," and his analysis "suggests that quality spread differentials exist because of factors that are not exploitable for economic gain." Wall and Pringle agree with his analysis with the exception of the possibility of agency savings as described earlier (1989, 62-64).

28 Their probit model was significant at the (p = 0.01) level based on a chi-square statistic of 13.26 with 3 degrees of freedom (Dhaliwal, *et al*, 51-52).

29 See Appendix B for disclosure requirements.

30 The provisions of SFAS 105 are applicable for financial statements issued for fiscal years ending after June 15, 1990.

31 Morck, *et al* (1988) use shareholdings of the board of directors as their primary measurement of management ownership.

<sup>32</sup> A different dependent variable was used in each of these studies. Each was hypothesized to vary systematically as a reflection of the owner/manager conflict. In the Morck, *et al* (1988) study, the dependent variable is Tobin's Q, representing market valuation of the firm, Francis and Wilson (1988) compare dependent variables representing two models of audit quality, and use the manager ownership (independent) variable as a proxy for agency costs related to the owner/manager conflict, and Niehaus (1989) uses the probability of a firm's using LIFO V.S. FIFO as the dependent variable, with both the level of management ownership and its square as independent variables.

<sup>33</sup> The "convergence" effect and "alignment" effect are defined and used as interchangable synonyms in this study.

<sup>34</sup> The measure of managers' ability to exercise control without being subject to the discipline of owners or their representatives has been termed entrenchment (Morck *et al* 1988) and also managerial discretion (Niehaus 1989). The terms are used here as interchangable and synonomous.

<sup>35</sup> This relationship is further complicated by the presence of intermediaries such as fund/portfolio managers whose interests are presumed to be aligned with those of the legal owners, but who may not attempt to discipline managers other than by selling the owners' stake.

<sup>36</sup> Morck, *et al* (1988, 301) itemize "conditions conducive to the entrenchment of incumbent management such as status as a founder, increased voting power, increased tenure with and attachment to the firm, lower employment of professional managers, and dominance of inside over outside directors" which may be associated with increases in managerial ownership.

<sup>37</sup> Dhaliwal, *et al* (1982) define firms with greater diffusion of ownership, or management-controlled firms, as those having no single party controlling a block of stock greater than 5%.

<sup>38</sup> This may be due in part to the use of 1980 data from Fortune 500 firms in both studies to construct tests of substantially the same theory. Both the dependent and independent variables in the models tested in the two studies were quite different, however.

# Chapter Three

# Hypothesis Specification, Research Methods and Design

Prior research in accounting provides a rationale for the examination of interest rate swap disclosures as well as guidance in the selection of variables and the design of tests. There are two obstacles to traditional testing for economic consequences of the quality of swap disclosure on non-management shareholders. One is the diversity of swap disclosures both in terms of substance and timing. This diversity precludes identification of an "event date" which could provide a benchmark for measuring market reaction, thus making the use of traditional market based event-study methods untenable. The other obstacle is the unobservable nature of managers' intentions. The result of managerial choices can be observed, however, in the form of the quality of the disclosures which they issue. The disclosures serve as a reflection of those managerial intentions which have been implemented, and are of immediate interest to users of financial information. Tests in this study are designed to examine cross-sectional association between a measure of swap disclosure quality (DSCQ) and selected attributes representing the ownership structure and the credit risk of the disclosing firms.

The general hypothesis to be tested in this study is:

CROSS SECTIONAL VARIATION IN THE QUALITY OF DISCLOSURES OF INTEREST RATE SWAP TRANS-ACTIONS IS ASSOCIATED WITH THE CREDIT RISK AND OWNERSHIP STRUCTURE OF THE DISCLOSING FIRMS.

Tests of specific associated hypotheses require the identification and measurement of a number of variables. The design of the study has been divided into four primary research tasks. These tasks include the development of: (1) a measure of disclosure quality, (2) a measure of credit risk, (3) measures of ownership structure, and (4) hypotheses to be tested using the variables which make up these measures in multinomial logit models.

The measure of disclosure quality (DSCQ), serves as the dependent variable and represents a measure of the quality of disclosure of swap transactions for an individual firm. The measures of credit risk (i.e. the ability of a firm to repay its debts) and ownership structure serve as the two categories of independent variables. These variables, the rationales for their selection and measurement, and the hypotheses to be tested are described below. The selection of the sample and the design of the tests of the research hypotheses are also described in the remainder of the chapter.

## THE DEPENDENT VARIABLE: DISCLOSURE QUALITY

The measure of disclosure quality (DSCQ) was developed in two steps. First, observations of actual disclosures in the firms' accounting reports were recorded in the form of a set of ten firm-specific attributes. The reports examined include the primary financial statements and associated footnotes and the Management's Discussion and Analysis in the firm's Annual Report and/or Form 10K, as well as the proxy statement. Each attribute represents a particular feature of that firm's interest rate swap disclosure as described below. A record was developed for each firm which indicates the presence or absence of each of the ten attributes in that firm's swap disclosure. This results in a score (ranging from 1 to 10) for each firm based upon a count of the number of attributes which appear in the firm's financial disclosures. The multinomial tests were conducted using three disclosure levels based on this score. The highest disclosure quality level (DSCQ=3) represents scores greater than 5, the mid-level exactly 5, and firms disclosing with low quality (DSCQ=1) disclosed fewer than 5 of the ten attributes.

*Disclosure Attributes*

The attributes to be used in measuring DSCQ were selected primarily based on the disclosure requirements and suggestions established in SFAS 105 (FASB 1990). The primary requirement applicable to interest rate swaps is:

> For financial instruments with off-balance-sheet risk, ..., an entity shall disclose either in the body of the financial statements or in the accompanying notes the following information...
>
> a. The face or contract amount (or notional principal amount if there is no face or contract amount)
>
> b. The nature and terms, including, at a minimum, a discussion of (1) the credit and market risk of those instruments, (2) the cash requirements of those instruments, and (3) the related accounting policy pursuant to the requirements of APB Opinion No. 22, *Disclosure of Accounting Policies.*

The FASB has provided an example (1990, Appendix C, Example 1) of an interest rate swap disclosure for a nonfinancial entity. Items in the example are considered important features of the swap for disclosure purposes, although some are not explicitly required. An example of this is the disclosure of a stated motive for engaging in swaps. Paragraph 94 states,

> a requirement to disclose the purpose of entering into certain financial instruments is not necessary because reporting entities are likely to disclose that information to explain more adequately the nature of risks of those instruments, if deemed necessary (FASB 1990).

Despite the lack of a requirement, the purpose for entering into swap agreements is included in the FASB's example of swap disclosure.

In addition to the nine attributes which are derived directly from SFAS 105, one attribute (see HEDGE below) discloses the firms purpose for using a swap and also appears in the "swaps" literature

(Bierman 1987; Nair, *et al* 1990). It records the disclosure of an intended relationship between the swap and the firm's other assets or liabilities. This disclosure indicates whether the swap was intended as a hedge of market movements in interest rates in addition to a swap of one type of debt for another. For example, while the swap allows the firm to exchange the terms of existing debt (e.g. floating for fixed) the resulting character of this liability is often intended to combine with the character of the firm's assets (also fixed) to better match required cash flows and thus hedge market changes in interest rate risk. Disclosure of a relationship between the swap and other assets or liabilities would reflect the change in overall market risk exposure of the firm which results from the swap. SFAS 105 requires a discussion of the market risk of financial instruments, but does not specifically address the swap-related change in the firm's overall market risk.

The ten attributes used to measure disclosure quality are listed below. The order in which they are listed is not intended to suggest a relative ranking or weighting of disclosure significance. Although some might argue that managers acting with guile might selectively withhold or include disclosure of certain features of swap transactions in order to mislead statement readers, no explanation of how this might be accomplished has been advanced in past research or on the part of standard setting bodies. Indeed, a manager's decision to disclose (or withhold) an attribute might be explained alternatively as acting with guile, or acting based on criteria such as materiality or cost effectiveness. In the absence of a theoretically defensible weighting scheme, each of the following disclosure attributes has been treated as bearing equally on the quality of disclosure:

NPRIN:     notional principal, individually or by class;

EFFINT:     effective interest rate on a particular portion of debt after considering the swap. (Note that this information implies a relationship between the swap and underlying debt);

TYPE:     the type of payments to be made or received under the swap (e.g. fixed or floating rate);

BASIS:     the basis for determining cash payments to be made and/or received. (e.g. floating rates based on LIBOR[39] or a fixed rate pegged to Treasury Notes);

EXP:     length or expiration date of the swap(s);

CRISK:     the existence of credit risk due to the potential for counterparty default on the swap agreement;

RECPOL:     policy with regard to recognition and disclosure of swap-related interest received/paid and/or premiums received/paid;

TERMPOL:     policy with regard to the accounting treatment of gains or losses on early termination of swaps;

LOC:     disclosure in the primary statements or notes (or incorporated into them by reference to a location within the same document per, FASB 1990 Appendix D, paragraph 122;

HEDGE:     use of the swap to hedge interest rate risk associated with assets or liabilities of the firm (other than any directly related debt which is effectively altered by the swap).

## INDEPENDENT VARIABLES: FIRM CREDIT RISK

The FASB has defined credit risk with regard to the risk of accounting loss from holding a financial instrument. It is described as:

the possibility that a loss may occur from the failure of another party to perform according to the terms of a contract, (FASB 1990, 3).

In this study, the definition of credit risk is substantially the same, but the focus is on the overall credit risk of the firm itself. It is distinct from, but encompasses, the credit risk arising from potential failure of counterparty firm(s) to perform under contract as described by the FASB. Credit risk and concentrations of credit risk as described by the FASB are important to the disclosing firm in assessing its expected cash inflows. That risk, however, is related specifically to the solvency and financial reliability of the counterparty. The issue of particular interest in this study is the overall measure of credit risk (i.e. credit worthiness from an investor or lender's point of view) of the disclosing firm.

## *Selection of Credit Risk Variables*

The accounting literature includes many studies in which the authors develop a model of bankruptcy or financial distress prediction, (e.g. Beaver, 1966; Altman, 1968; Ohlson, 1980; Zavgren, 1985; Lau, 1987; Altman, Haldeman, and Narayanan, 1977) or of loan or bond rating classification (e.g. Marais, Patell, & Wolfson, 1984; Dietrich & Kaplan, 1982; Kaplan & Urwitz 1979). The selection of variables used to measure credit risk is subjective and is often based on results of past studies and practical experience. As Marais, *et al*, explain,

> Because there exists no well-developed theory of loan difficulty to guide the selection of...variables, most studies (including ours) proceed heuristically, selecting variables suggested by practitioners or by empirical search techniques. Bankruptcy and bond-rating studies typically focus on financial statement data taken from the Compustat tapes, although some have incorporated nonaccounting information such as stock prices (1984, 94).

Beaver also describes the criteria he used to:

> select...ratios from the set of all possible combinations and permutations of financial statement items. The three

criteria were: popularity-frequent appearance in the literature,; the ratios performed well in one of the previous studies, and the ratio was definable in terms of a "cash flow" concept (1966, 78-79).

Ohlson reports that in his study,

> No attempt was made to select predictors on the basis of rigorous theory. To put it mildly, the state of the art seems to preclude such an approach...predictors were partially selected simply because they appear to be the ones most frequently mentioned in the literature (1980, 118, note 10).

Credit risk variables used in this study were selected based on their frequent use in the literature, and on their use in past studies to test for solvency. A firm's ability to maintain its credit standing provided the focus for selection. For example, two variables, stock and dividend flexibility (SKFX and DIV), serve as measures of a firm's financial flexibility,[40] (Lau, 1987; Heath, 1978; FASB, 1980; Donaldson, 1986). In those past studies, they were used to capture the firm's ability to maintain a state of solvency in the face of unexpected events.

A set of non-financial statement variables is included for similar reasons. That is, they were taken from a study in which the focus was loan classification rather than bankruptcy prediction. Marais, *et al* (1984) found that a set of non-financial statement variables used in their study performed as well as a larger set of financial statement variables in the loan classification process. They interpreted this result as an indication that market related information like debt ratings and the variability of stock prices can effectively substitute for or summarize the results of extensive financial statement analysis. Three market related (non-financial statement) variables used by Marais, *et al* are used in this study, and three more are collapsed into one debt rating variable. An additional market variable which has been associated with bond ratings in past studies (e.g. Kaplan and Urwitz 1979) is the firm's Beta. The Beta is a measure of the systematic risk of the firm's common stock, and has also been included in the current study.

The variables used in this study to measure the credit riskiness of firms are listed below. Authors in whose studies they were included are shown in brackets.  Acronyms used to identify the variables are shown in capital letters.

## Liquidity:

Quick Assets / Current Liabilities          **QUICK**
(Zavgren; Marais, Patell, & Wolfson; Mensah; Beaver)

Current Ratio[41]                                **CURR**
(Marais, *et al*; Mensah; Altman, Haldeman & Narayanan; Beaver)

Working Capital / Total Assets               **WCTA**
(Marais, *et al*; Mensah; Ohlson; Altman; Altman, *et al*; Beaver)

Cash / Total Assets                              **CTA**
(Zavgren; Marais, *et al*; Beaver)

Cash Flow / Total Liabilities              **CFTL**
(Lau;[42] Marais, *et al*;[43] Mensah; Kaplan and Urwitz;[44] Altman, *et al*; Beaver)

## Leverage:

Debt / Equity                                      **DE**
(Zavgren; Ziebart)

Debt / Assets                                      **DA**
(Mensah; Ohlson; Beaver; Marais, *et al*)

## Profitability:

Net Income / Total Capital            **NICAP**
(Zavgren; Mensah; Beaver)

Net Income / Total Assets          **NITA**
(Marais, *et al*; Ohlson; Kaplan & Urwitz; Beaver; Ziebart)

## Stock flexibility:

Stock Price Trend: $\dfrac{(H_t - H_{t-1}) + (L_t - L_{t-1})}{H_t + H_{t-1} + L_t + L_{t-1}}$     **SKFX**

($H_t$ and $L_t$ are respectively, the high and low values of the range of stock prices in year t)   (Lau)

## Dividend flexibility:           DIV

1                  if no dividend is being paid currently,
0                                   otherwise
(Lau; Marais *et al*)

## Non-Financial Statement Variables:

Debt-Rating Variable          **DRAT**
1                  if commercial paper is rated P-1 or P-2
                       and all publicly traded debt outstanding
                       is investment grade
0                                   otherwise
(combines variables of Marais, *et al*)

Stock Exchange Indicator                          **EXC**
1                    if traded on the New York Stock Exchange
0                                                    otherwise
(Marais, *et al*)


Standard Deviation of                             **STDEV**
Weekly Returns on Common Stock
(Marais, *et al*)


Beta:                                             **BETA**
(Kaplan & Urwitz)


Size:                                             **TOTASSET**
Total Assets
(Ohlson; Kaplan & Urwitz; Altman, *et al*)


## CONFIRMATORY FACTOR ANALYSIS (CFA)
## MODEL OF CREDIT RISK

In credit risk or bankruptcy prediction models, the independent variables used are often classified into groups which represent latent (unobservable) variables, often called factors. Many of the variables above have been classified in this way in past studies as noted by the group titles. Liquidity, for example, is a latent variable or factor which has been represented (measured) by the first five observable variables.   Generally, latent variables represent some characteristic of the entity under study which has traditionally been recognized as an important feature but which is too complex to be measured directly.

An example of the use of Confirmatory Factor Analysis (CFA) in a context similar to the current study is provided by Ziebart (1983). He attempted to develop and test a model to provide evidence that groups of financial variables traditionally used to represent factors such as liquidity were present in financial data. His study was also designed to concurrently test for the information content of these factors in financial disclosures of a set of firms. Ziebart (1983) used

CFA to evaluate a model in which a set of accounting variables was used to represent each of four economic factors. These factors were thought to be generally useful to investors for evaluating individual firms. Tests using CFA are similar to traditional factor analysis except that the theorized relationships (or unrelatedness) between variables and factors are specified at the outset, and testing is based upon that specific set of expected relationships (as described more fully in Chapter 4.) This differs from traditional factor analysis in which relationships are identified by the factor analysis, rather than confirmed or rejected by it (Long 1983).

Three of the four factors in Ziebart's 1983 study (liquidity, leverage, and profitability) were also present in the bankruptcy studies of Ohlson (1980) and Altman (1968) and are used to classify some of the credit risk variables in this study. Although Ziebart's data did not support the factor structure in his proposed measurement model, he subsequently developed an alternative model linking each of the observed variables individually to market reactions. That model proved to have a very high level of fit (p=0.997), (Ziebart 1983, 117).

There are three important implications for this study in Ziebart's (1983) work. First, the potential exists for development of a model which includes the measurement of latent variables in predicting firm performance. Second, the variables and factors selected for his study were drawn from those traditionally recognized in the literature as was done in this study. Even though Ziebart's proposed factor model was not confirmed, future research designs based on such precedents may eventually be successful in developing this type of model. Third, Ziebart's work confirms the importance of variables traditionally associated with credit risk in that they are associated with market reactions. The reactions of the market, in turn, determine changes in shareholders' wealth.

CFA is used in this study to test the goodness of fit of an initial model of credit risk, as well as to test the fit of a credit risk measurement model developed in a more exploratory manner. The initial model includes all of the accounting and non-accounting variables listed above. Subsequent models have been revised in ways which rely primarily on the interpretation of findings in prior tests.

CFA has often been used, by Ziebart (1983), for example, in an exploratory sense to revise a model based on the empirical evidence at hand. Assuming that model revisions are theoretically defensible, this process results in a reduction of the number of observed variables used to measure latent variables. CFA is based upon the expectation that observed variables which serve as measures of latent variables will be significantly correlated with one another and at the same time, less highly correlated with variables which serve as measures of other latent variables. Model revision often proceeds by removing those variables which don't exhibit predicted patterns of correlation with other variables in the model, thereby arriving at a more parsimonious model.

Use of CFA in an exploratory fashion which results in a model which is both parsimonious and theoretically defensible is still subject to the charge that the model is dependent on the particular set of data used to develop it. One method of increasing the external validity of the results would be to randomly divide the data into two sub-samples, one used for exploratory procedures, and a holdout sample used to confirm the results of the initial tests. In this study, the size of the data set precludes this type of analytical confirmation of the model. In addition, such a procedure would still be subject to the charge that the data, even if randomly subdivided, is specific to swap-disclosing firms and thus not strictly reliable for development of a general model of credit risk.

The objective of this part of the study is to develop a measure which can be interpreted as capturing the riskiness of the firms in this data set. The historical precedents listed above in which various subsets of these accounting and market related variables were repeatedly chosen to represent the riskiness of firms, and their significance across a variety of research designs, are cited as evidence of the external validity of the resulting measures.

# INDEPENDENT VARIABLES

*Ownership Structure*

The ownership structure variables were chosen for their potential in serving as measures either of managerial discretion (entrenchment) or the ability of outside owners to monitor and discipline managers.

MGR: THE PERCENTAGE OF COMMON SHARES HELD BY MANAGERS AND DIRECTORS OF THE FIRM AND REPRESENTS THE LEVEL OF

CONCENTRATION OF OWNERSHIP WHICH IS IN THE HANDS OF MANAGEMENT.

OC:     A DICHOTOMOUS VARIABLE REPRESENTING OWNER CONTROL, CODED ONE IF THE LARGEST OWNER HOLDS 5% OR MORE[45] OF THE OUTSTANDING COMMON SHARES AND ZERO OTHERWISE.

NOSH:THE NUMBER OF COMMON SHAREHOLDERS IN THE FIRM, A MEASURE OF THE DIFFUSION OF OWNERSHIP.

These variables provide a basis for testing the following three hypotheses about how they relate to the quality of interest rate swap disclosures. Tests of these hypotheses will be incorporated into the multinomial logit model described below.

*Managerial Ownership*

$H_1$:     THE QUALITY OF INTEREST RATE SWAP DISCLOSURES DSCQ WILL VARY AS THE PERCENTAGE OF MANAGERIAL OWNERSHIP MGR INCREASES IN A MANNER WHICH IS DETERMINED BY THE DOMINANCE OF EITHER THE CONVERGENCE OF INTERESTS EFFECT OR THE ENTRENCHMENT EFFECT

MGR is used as a measure of managerial ownership. It is used to test for the opposing effects of the convergence of interests and management entrenchment (Morck, *et al* 1988). The test is appropriate for this study because swap-related conflicts of interests arise as a result of managers' private information. If managers are privately aware that a swap and short term debt would injure their interests as shareholders, the probability that they will take such action is expected to diminish as their ownership share increases. *At some point, maximization of firm value would become more valuable to the owner-manager than the benefits of higher currently reported income.* Accordingly, as the interests of managers converge with those of owners, swaps to fix debt payments are less likely to give rise to agency costs. The associated incentive to avoid clear disclosure is expected to decrease as MGR increases.

The variable MGR also serves as a measure of managerial entrenchment and control. As managers' ownership stake in the firm becomes proportionally larger than that of outside owners, managers are more likely to be able to obtain entrepreneurial gains (e.g. provide themselves with bonuses or large salaries) without being subjected to discipline by outside owners.

The test of managerial ownership is designed to detect evidence of a non-linear (quadratic) relationship between DSCQ and MGR in the sample data. The analysis will include both MGR and $MGR^2$ as independent variables. As described in Niehaus' (1989) study, if the entrenchment effect is dominant over the lower range of managerial ownership and the convergence of interests effect dominates over the higher range, the expected results in a dichotomous logit analysis would be a negative coefficient for MGR and a positive coefficient for $MGR^2$. If the convergence of interests effect dominates over the entire range of managerial ownership both coefficients would be positive, and both would be negative if entrenchment is always dominant. In a multinomial logit model in which the dependent variable takes more than two values, interpretation of the results is less straightforward. This is due to the fact that the signs of the coefficients are not sufficient to determine the direction of change of the corresponding (disclosure) probabilities (Aldrich and Nelson 1984). Interpretation of the multinomial logit model is described in more detail in Chapter 4.

*Owner Control*

$H_2$:     THE QUALITY OF INTEREST RATE SWAP DISCLOSURES DSCQ WILL BE POSITIVELY RELATED TO OWNER

## CONTROL OC ACROSS SWAP-DISCLOSING FIRMS.

OC serves to identify a firm in which managers are most likely to be subject to the monitoring and discipline of owners. The rationale behind the use of this variable in the current study is that firms for which OC is zero have a relatively diffuse ownership in the sense that no one owner holds a sufficiently large stake to exercise effective control over the management of the firm.

OC is a measure which has been used in several prior studies. It is very similar to that used by Dhaliwal, *et al* (1982) to distinguish between MC (manager-controlled) and OC firms. In their study, they classify firms as OC if one party owned 10% or more of the voting stock and exercised active control, or if one party owned 20% or more of the voting stock. A 10% owner who also was a manager or director was categorized as exercising active control. Firms in their study were classified as MC when, "no single block of stock greater than 5 percent was controlled by any party" (Dhaliwal *et al* 1982, 48).

In the current study, the level at which OC is coded 1 has been decreased to 5% to coincide with the ownership threshold below which Dhaliwal *et al* (1982) classified firms as MC. It also is considered appropriate because 5% is the level of ownership at which the SEC requires disclosure (Regulation S-K, Item 403, Subpart 229.403) with regard to the amount of stock owned by a particular shareholder.

*Number of Shareholders*

$H_3$:    THE QUALITY OF INTEREST RATE SWAP DISCLOSURES DSCQ WILL DECREASE AS THE NUMBER OF SHAREHOLDERS NOSH INCREASES ACROSS SWAP-DISCLOSING FIRMS.

NOSH is a measure of the diffusion of ownership over a population of shareholders. As the size of the group of shareholders increases, the expense and amount of effort each must incur in order to carry out effective monitoring and disciplining of management is expected to increase, and the associated rewards to individual shareholders to diminish, accordingly. The expected result of increases in the number of shareholders, then, is a decrease in effective monitoring and an increase in management discretion. This is also consistent with the characterization of NOSH as a measure of firm size later in the study, as explained in Chapter 4. In general, the number of shareholders increases with the size of the firm, and diffusion of ownership would be expected to increase with firm size. As described in greater detail in Chapter 4, studies of the ownership structure of firms have generally included a control for the size of the firm.

*Firm Size and Leverage*

Dhaliwal *et al* (1982) cite evidence in past accounting research which suggests that accounting choices (e.g. the choice of accounting methods) are consistently influenced by the size (Watts and Zimmerman, 1978; Hagerman and Zmijewski, 1979) and leverage (Dhaliwal, 1980; Bowen *et al*, 1982) of the firm. Accordingly, past studies of ownership structure control for the effects of size and leverage in the research design (Dhaliwal *et al*, 1982; Francis and Wilson, 1988; Niehaus, 1989).

In this study, independent variables representative of both size (LNASSETS, EXC) and leverage (DE, DA) are included in the group of credit risk variables. In addition, the variable NOSH, used as a measure of the diffusion of ownership, is also generally representative of the size of the firm.

## MULTINOMIAL LOGIT ANALYSIS: THE GENERAL HYPOTHESIS

The general hypothesis for this study, also stated at the beginning of this chapter, is:

CROSS SECTIONAL VARIATION IN THE QUALITY OF DISCLOSURES OF INTEREST RATE SWAP TRANS- ACTIONS IS ASSOCIATED WITH THE CREDIT RISK AND OWNERSHIP STRUCTURE OF THE DISCLOSING FIRMS.

It is tested using a multinomial logit model, (McFadden, 1974; Ohlson, 1980; Amemiya, 1981; Lau, 1987; Maddala, 1983, Aldrich and Nelson, 1984) with DSCQ as the discrete (polychotomous) dependent variable, as follows:

$$\text{PROB } [\text{DSCQ}] = A + B_1 \text{ MGR} + B_2 \text{ MGR}^2 + B_3 \text{ OC} + B_4 \text{ NOSH} + (B_5...B_N) \text{ CREDIT RISK VARIABLES}$$

The set of credit risk variables included in the model was determined based on the results of confirmatory factor analysis. In general, CFA allows for the computation of factor scores across observations for each of the latent variables (e.g. liquidity, leverage, profitability and size). These scores can then be used as independent variables (representing size, etc.) in subsequent analyses. The use of factor scores to represent the credit risk variables in this study is supported both by the use of the underlying observed variables in past studies of credit risk (as described earlier), and by the goodness of fit of the corresponding CFA model (as presented in Chapter 4).

Multinomial logit analysis was developed in the 1960s, (see McFadden 1974). It has been attributed to a number of researchers, including McFadden, who is most often cited as the source for a comprehensive analysis of the models (e.g. Ohlson 1980, 118; Lau 1987, 133; Barniv 1990, 584). The conditional logit model employed by Ohlson (1980) and developed by McFadden (1974) is a variation of the multinomial logit model and was derived "from a theory of population choice behavior" (McFadden 1974, 114) and random utility models. Algebraically, the multinomial logit and conditional logit models are equivalent (Maddala 1983, 42).

The use of the multinomial (Lau 1987) or conditional logit model (Ohlson 1980; Burgstahler *et al* 1989) in studies of bankruptcy and credit risk has become more frequent since the publication of Ohlson's study in 1980. Ohlson justifies his choice of this model over Multivariate Discriminant Analysis (MDA), the method used most commonly in prior bankruptcy studies. Arguments advanced by Ohlson and in subsequent studies include:

(1)     Assumptions regarding the variables (e.g. that they are normally distributed) which are requirements of MDA are violated when qualitative (particularly

dichotomous) variables are included in the study. These assumptions are not required when using the logit models.

(2)     The output of the MDA model is a classification of observations into groups, whereas the logit models allow coefficients of individual variables to be tested for statistical significance

(3)     The logit models allow for probabilistic interpretation. (For example, in the current study, the results can be interpreted as the probability with which a certain firm issues reports with a particular level of DSCQ).

# IDENTIFICATION OF FIRMS TO BE INCLUDED IN THE STUDY

*The Data Set*

Firms disclosing swaps were identified using keyword searches of the National Automated Accounting Research System (NAARS) database maintained by the American Institute of Certified Public Accountants (AICPA) as well as the Compact Disclosure database. These searches identified firms having the phrases "interest rate swap" or "interest rate exchange" in either the primary financial statements including footnotes, or in the Management's Discussion and Analysis (required by SEC Regulation S-K, Item 303). The initial sample was reduced through the use of three discriminators.

*Discriminator 1*

Only those firms whose voting securities are publicly traded are included in the study. Financial disclosure is provided for the benefit of interested parties outside the firm who do not have direct access to firm-specific information. This study is primarily concerned with the potential adverse effects of limited disclosure on shareholders and investors who do not have private access to the firm's financial information.

*Discriminator 2*

The sample was also restricted by excluding those firms having primary Standard Industrial Classification (SIC) codes indicating that their primary economic activity is in finance, insurance and real estate.[46] This eliminated the group of firms for which earning fees by serving as a swap intermediary is likely to provide an economic motive for engaging in swap activity.

*Discriminator 3*

Firms disclosing interest rate swap transactions in annual reports for fiscal years ending between November 30, 1987 and April 30, 1989, and for which data for all variables was available to this researcher, have been included. This period begins with the issuance of the initial FASB Exposure Draft dealing with swaps and omits financial reports which are likely to have been prepared and issued after the publication of the revised exposure draft on July 21, 1989. It is likely that cross-sectional variation in firms' disclosures prior to or after this period represents responses to new information about potential FASB disclosure guidelines as well as the effects of credit riskiness and ownership structure. Testing between periods of official regulatory activity serves as a control for this potential alternative explanation.

*Data Sources*

The financial statement variables were obtained either from financial databases (primarily the Compustat Industrial tapes, or infrequently from NAARS, or Compact Disclosure) or directly from firms' financial statements (in Annual Reports or SEC Forms 10K). In cases in which original published financial statements were available the data was matched against items from the databases to confirm the reliability of those sources. Data representing non-financial statement variables was gathered from various publicly available sources as in past studies using comparable variables. *Moody's Bond Record* is the source for bond ratings for companies holding rated debt. BETA was obtained from *Standard and Poor's Stock Guide*. The daily stock returns data for calculating the returns volatility variable STDEV was obtained from the Center for Research in Security Prices (CRSP) tapes.

Ownership data has been obtained from individual firms' Forms 10K or Proxy Statements, or in a few cases, research databases (NAARS and Compustat) which report data taken from those same public documents.

In this chapter the research questions and hypotheses tested in this study have been presented. The design of the study has been divided into four primary research tasks.

The first is the development of a measure of disclosure quality, DSCQ. The measure consists of a count of the number of a given set of disclosure attributes which are observed and recorded for each firm in the study. The firms are then classified into groups based upon their resulting DSCQ scores. The primary evidence of a high quality disclosure is the number of attributes disclosed. The ranking (from 1 to 3) of the group into which an observation (firm) has been classified serves as the dependent variable DSCQ in subsequent tests.

The second task is the development of a model of credit risk. The variables to be included in this model, and their origins, are listed. In the absense of a rigorous theory of credit risk or bankruptcy, they have been selected based upon their use in past studies. These variables are used as the empirical base for the development of the credit risk model using confirmatory factor analysis. Confirmation of the proposed factor model provides assurance that the observed variables selected for the study measure a set of latent variables which can be interpreted as representing credit risk.

The third task is the selection of variables used to measure and test ownership structure. The variables used, the rationales for their selection, and the forms in which they enter the subsequent multinomial logit analysis are explained.

The final research task in the study is the testing of the general hypothesis using multinomial logit analysis. A brief description of multinomial logit analysis was presented. A more detailed description of the tests performed, and the presentation and analysis of the results, are included in the next chapter.

# Notes

[39] LIBOR is the London Interbank Offered Rate and often serves either as the floating rate or a benchmark for the floating rate interest payments determined in a swap. The ISDA *Code of Standard Wording, Assumptions and Provisions for Swaps* (1986, vii) lists six floating rate options other than LIBOR. They are: Prime, Treasury Bill, Certificate of Deposit, Commercial Paper, Federal Funds, and Bankers Acceptance.

[40] Heath, (1978, 20) defines a financially flexible company, "as one that can take corrective action that will eliminate an excess of required cash payments over expected cash receipts quickly and with minor adverse effect on present or future earnings or on the market value of its stock."and cites the similarity of his use of the term with Donaldson's (1986) concept of financial mobility. Lau (1987, 129) cites both of these authors and the financial flexibility concept as having provided the basis for her selection of explanatory variables.

[41] The current ratio is of special interest in this study. The use of swaps and short-term debt to replace long term debt allows managers the potential to manipulate the current ratio. This is the case because the short-term debt, when paired with the swap, will be renewed, or rolled over each period. In these cases, *Statement of Financial Accounting Standards No. 6* (FASB 1975) allows firms to classify such short-term obligations as long-term financing. This may aid managers who must comply with debt covenants establishing a minimum current ratio to utilize short debt maturities without changing the current ratio. Since the current ratio remains unchanged, this type of activity would not be detected by tests of credit risk, but firms with a higher current ratio are more likely to engage in this activity.

[42] Lau (1987, 130) uses working capital flow / total debt to proxy for borrowing capacity.

[43] Marais, *et al* (1984, 94) use funds flow / total liabilities.

[44] Kaplan and Urwitz (1979) use cash flow before interest and taxes / total debt.

[45] SEC Regulation S-K requires disclosure of beneficial ownership of more than 5%. A disclosure of exactly 5% ownership is classified as OC = 1 since with rounding, this is likely to represent slightly more than 5% and, since it has been disclosed, to meet the spirit of the requirement.

---

[46] Three digit primary SIC codes for which the first two digits are 60 through 67 are excluded.

# Chapter Four

# Analysis and Interpretation of Research Results

## INTRODUCTION

In this chapter, organization and detail of the analysis performed in the study are discussed. Some commentary with regard to the results of statistical tests is provided, although the presentation of conclusions is largely reserved for Chapter 5. As indicated in earlier chapters, the project encompassed four primary research tasks. A discussion of the performance of those tasks, (1) the measurement of DSCQ, (2) the development of a set of independent variables to represent credit risk using a Confirmatory Factor Analysis, (3) the selection of independent variables to be included in the ownership structure model, and (4) testing of the resulting models using multinomial logit analysis, again serves to organize the discussion in this chapter. The discussion is modified in that the first and third tasks required no additional analysis and are treated briefly at the start of the chapter.

The second task, involving CFA, is treated in much greater detail. The independent variables resulting from the first three tasks are then combined in several multinomial logit models. The tests, findings and analyses for these models, comprising the fourth research task, is presented sequentially. The full model, including the credit risk variables, is presented first. Then, models designed specifically to test ownership structure are presented. A data set representing 63 additional firms was available for tests of ownership structure. Results of the analysis of ownership structure models for both data sets (102 and 63), as well as a pooled sample, are reported.

# DATA COLLECTION AND MEASUREMENT OF DISCLOSURE QUALITY

The first step in the analysis for this project was collection of the data. As noted earlier, the firms were identified using keyword searches of the NAARS and Compact Disclosure databases. It was then necessary to obtain the firm-specific data items required for testing. The list of 102 firms for which all independent variables were available is presented in Appendix C, with selected variable values. Sufficient information for testing multinomial logit models of ownership structure was available for an additional 63 firms. The names and data values for these firms are also presented in Appendix C. For each of these 165 firms, a measure of DSCQ was developed through a complete reading of the firm's financial statements (including associated footnotes) and the Management Discussion and Analysis in the firm's Annual Report or Form 10K. The collection of disclosure items and subsequent development of the three-level dependent variable, DSCQ was described in Chapter 3 and required no further analysis. The resulting measure of disclosure quality for each firm is also presented in Appendix C.

# CONFIRMATORY FACTOR ANALYSIS

*A Model of Credit Risk*

CFA was used initially to test a model which included all of the credit risk variables described in Chapter 3. These variables are shown again below grouped to represent the four factors (latent variables) initially hypothesized to represent credit risk. This set of factors is based upon the characterization of the variables in prior studies. The sources and computations used to calculate the observed variables are listed.

# LIQUIDITY:

### QUICK
(Cash + Total Receivables) / Current Liabilities

## CURR
Current Assets / Current Liabilities

## WCTA
(Current Assets - Current Liabilities) / Total Assets

## CTA
Natural Log of: Cash / Total Assets[47]

## CFTL
Total Cash Flow[48] / Total Liabilities

## SKFX
Given that $H_t$ and $L_t$ are the high and low common share prices in year t:

$$\frac{(H_t - H_{t-1}) + (L_t - L_{t-1})}{H_t + H_{t-1} + L_t + L_{t-1}}$$

## DRAT
1        if outstanding commercial paper or bonds are rated as investment grade,

0        otherwise[49]

# LEVERAGE

## DE
Total Liabilities / Total Equity

## DA
Natural log of: Total Liabilities / Total Assets

## PROFITABILITY

### NICAP
Net Income / Equity + Deferred Tax

### NITA
Net Income / Total Assets

### DIV
1        if a dividend was issued in the current year,

0        otherwise

### STDEV
Natural log of the standard deviation of weekly returns on
Common Stock

### BETA
Beta published in *Standard & Poors Stock Reports*

## SIZE

### LNASSET
The natural log of Total Assets

### EXC
1        if the firm is listed on the New York Stock
         Exchange

0        otherwise

Confirmatory Factor Analysis begins with the computation of a matrix of correlations between the variables in the model. Correlations (rather than covariances) are used here despite the loss of information which occurs when variables are standardized. The variables in this study are not all measured on a common scale, which makes the use of correlations (standardization) necessary for comparability (Loehlin 1987). Since the data set to be analyzed includes several dichotomous variables, the correlation matrix includes a mixture of product moment correlations (for pairs in which both variables are continuous), polychoric correlations (for pairs in which both variables are dichotomous) and polyserial correlations for mixed pairs (Joreskog and Sorbom 1989; Olsson 1979; Olsson, Drasgow and Dorans 1982; Muthen 1984).[50]

Correlations between the observed variables serve as input in the estimation of a factor analytic "measurement model" which was developed by Joreskog (1978) and implemented in the program LISREL (Analysis of Linear Structural Relationships) by Joreskog and Sorbom (1989). The initial measurement model for this study, illustrated below in a path diagram (Figure 2) using the notation of Joreskog and Sorbom,[51] consists of a set of measurement equations (described in Figure 2) which is solved iteratively. Of the several methods of estimation available, Maximum Likelihood (ML) and Generalized Least Squares (GLS) estimation are used in this study to estimate the parameters of the model. Two sets of estimates are computed in order to provide additional evidence that the resulting measures of latent variables are not due to spurious effects of a particular fitting function (Loehlin 1987).

CFA of the four-factor credit risk model, as originally proposed and depicted in Figure 2, was not successful. Using each fitting function in turn, the proposed model failed to converge after 80 iterations, whereas Joreskog and Sorbom (1989) advise that a solution which does not converge after 10 iterations generally will not. This is indicative of a poorly specified model. Accordingly, respecification of the model was undertaken, with redesign of the model based on the following lines of reasoning:

| Figure 2 | INITIAL CFA MEASUREMENT MODEL | | |
|---|---|---|---|
| error terms: | observed variables: | factor loadings: | latent variables: |
| $delta_1$ | QUICK $(x_1)$ | $lambda_{11}$ | |
| $delta_2$ | CURR $(x_2)$ | $lambda_{21}$ | |
| $delta_3$ | WCTA $(x_3)$ | $lambda_{31}$ | |
| $delta_4$ | CTA $(x_4)$ | $lambda_{41}$ | $ksi_1$: |
| $delta_5$ | CFTL $(x_5)$ | $lambda_{51}$ | LIQUIDITY |
| $delta_6$ | SKFX $(x_6)$ | $lambda_{61}$ | |
| $delta_7$ | DRAT $(x_7)$ | $lambda_{71}$ | |
| | | | |
| $delta_8$ | DE $(x_8)$ | $lambda_{82}$ | $ksi_2$: |
| $delta_9$ | DA $(x_9)$ | $lambda_{92}$ | LEVERAGE |
| | | | |
| $delta_{10}$ | NICAP $(x_{10})$ | $lambda_{103}$ | |
| $delta_{11}$ | NITA $(x_{11})$ | $lambda_{113}$ | $ksi_3$: |
| $delta_{12}$ | DIV $(x_{12})$ | $lambda_{123}$ | PROFITABILITY |
| $delta_{13}$ | STDEV $(x_{13})$ | $lambda_{133}$ | |
| $delta_{14}$ | BETA $(x_{14})$ | $lambda_{143}$ | |
| | | | |
| $delta_{15}$ | EXC $(x_{15})$ | $lambda_{154}$ | $ksi_4$: |
| $delta_{16}$ | LNASSET $(x_{16})$ | $lambda_{164}$ | SIZE |

MATRIX FORMULATION OF MEASUREMENT EQUATIONS:

$$x_i = lambda_{ij} * ksi_j + delta_i$$

where:

$x_i$ is an i by 1 vector of observed variables

$lambda_{ij}$ is an i by j matrix of factor loadings

$ksi_j$ is a j by 1 vector of latent variables

$delta_i$ is an i by 1 vector of measurement errors on $x_i$

(1)      Many of the past studies from which the list of credit risk variables originated used a smaller subset of variables (e.g. Ohlson 1980 (9 variables), Zavgren 1985 (7 variables)). The use of fewer variables in this study is also more in keeping with the available sample size of 102 and the limitations of CFA. While the issue of the

appropriate sample size for CFA is often debated, and 100 observations is often considered adequate (Bagozzi and Yi 1988), Bentler (1985) has recommended a 5 to 1 ratio for sample observations to estimated parameters. Since the initial 16-variable model requires the estimation of 38 parameters[52], a model which specifies fewer variables, and thus fewer parameter estimates, is preferable.

(2)      The use of variables which measure liquidity are less likely than the others to be appropriate for the current study. This is because the study does not focus primarily on bankruptcy. While a lack of liquidity may be characteristic of firms in serious financial trouble, healthy firms are likely to minimize liquidity in order to maximize profitable investment. Healthy firms are also likely to have more resources available in the face of an unexpected cash shortage, reducing the need to maintain a highly liquid position. Also, the accumulation of unsold inventory by firms in trouble may increase indicators such as CURR or WCTA, making them ambiguous risk indicators (Zavgren 1985). Accordingly, variables used to measure liquidity (QUICK CURR WCTA CTA CFTL SKFX) were dropped from the model. The one exception is DRAT. Because it represents a credit rating, and thus a more general measure of credit risk than the others (as opposed to specifically measuring liquidity), it has been retained.

(3)      Although the variables NICAP and NITA were significantly correlated (.504, p=0.00) they were not included in the revised model. This pair of profitability measures was omitted due to a potential alternative explanation for their correlation: net income is the numerator in both ratios.

(4)      Finally, rather than simply selecting and categorizing the variables as they have been in the literature, those to be retained were selected in the context of a newly formulated model of credit risk. The new model is based on the perspectives of the two outside groups most likely to have an interest in the firm's disclosures: investors and creditors. BETA and STDEV, market-related variables which are closely associated with the systematic risk of a firm, were selected as variables of interest to investors. Creditors are also expected to have an interest in the credit riskiness of firms. Since creditors' claims are generally tied directly to the firm, with few market indicators to guide them in their evaluation of their investment, their interests are better captured by variables which are easily observed, but most closely associated with the unique risk of the firm. DRAT and DIV were

selected to represent measures of unique risk. The variables LNASSET and EXC, representing firm size, were retained from the original model. An additional measure, NOSH, was added to complete the third factor. The restated model, with proposed latent variables UNIQUE, MKT, and SIZE, is shown in Figure 3.

| Figure 3 | REVISED CFA MEASUREMENT MODEL | | |
|---|---|---|---|
| error terms: | observed variables: | factor loadings: | latent variables: |
| $delta_1$ | DRAT ($x_1$) | $lambda_{11}$ | $ksi_1$ |
| $delta_2$ | DIV ($x_2$) | $lambda_{21}$ | UNIQUE |
| | | | |
| $delta_3$ | BETA ($x_3$) | $lambda_{32}$ | $ksi_2$ |
| $delta_4$ | STDEV ($x_4$) | $lambda_{42}$ | MKT |
| | | | |
| $delta_5$ | NOSH ($x_5$) | $lambda_{53}$ | $ksi_3$ |
| $delta_6$ | EXC ($x_6$) | $lambda_{63}$ | SIZE |
| $delta_7$ | LNASSET ($x_7$) | $lambda_{73}$ | |

MATRIX FORMULATION OF MEASUREMENT EQUATIONS:

$$x_i = lambda_{ij} * ksi_j + delta_i$$

where:

$x_i$ is an  i by 1  vector of observed variables
$lambda_{ij}$ is an  i by j  matrix of factor loadings
ksi is a  j by 1  vector of latent variables
$delta_i$ is an i by 1 vector of measurement errors on $x_i$

*Evaluation of Measurement Models:  Goodness of Fit*

In CFA, the initial correlation matrix is compared with a new "reproduced" correlation matrix. This new matrix is computed using the parameters estimated in the measurement model. If the relationships among the variables which have been hypothesized and specified in the measurement model are present in the original data, then the new matrix (which is produced based on those specifications) will be similar to the original matrix. The similarity of the original and "reproduced" correlation matrices, then, provides a basis for assessing the goodness of fit of the estimated model.

Several indicators are commonly used to assess goodness of fit. One indicator is a $X^2$ test of the hypothesis that the original correlation matrix does not exhibit (or is "unconstrained" by) the proposed relationships (Joreskog and Sorbom 1989; Bagozzi and Yi 1988). The usefulness of the $X^2$ test is limited in several respects, however. For example, since it is calculated as (N-1) times the minimum value of the fitting function (i.e. ML or GLS) obtained for the model (where N is the number of observations in the sample), it is a function of the sample size. As sample size increases it is increasingly likely to indicate rejection of a model, irrespective of the validity of the model (Bagozzi and Yi 1988, Anderson and Gerbing 1984, Fornell and Larcker 1981, Bentler and Bonett 1980). Another problem is that the power of the $X^2$ test (the probability with which it will reject the null hypothesis when it is false) is not known (Fornell and Larcker 1981, Fornell 1983). This problem is compounded by the reversal of the traditional role of hypothesis testing as described by Fornell and Larcker (1981). Generally in significance testing, when the null hypothesis is rejected (i.e. the $X^2$ value is high and the significance level low), the theory is supported. In the testing for goodness of fit of CFA measurement models, however, rejection of the null hypothesis (which is that the correlation matrix is constrained in the predicted ways) in favor of the alternative hypothesis (that the original matrix is unconstrained) also represents a rejection of the proposed relationships. When the power of the test is low, the null hypothesis will not be rejected very often, and the probability of accepting a false theory will be greater.

The types of problems cited above, as well as the restrictive assumptions underlying the use of $X^2$ as a test statistic,[53] have led to its use as a,

> goodness-of-fit (or badness of fit) measure in the sense that large $X^2$-values correspond to bad fit and small $X^2$-values to good fit. The degrees of freedom serves as a standard by which to judge whether $X^2$ is large or small, (Joreskog and Sorbom 1989, 26).

Loehlin (1987) suggests as a rule of thumb, that a range of about 1-2 for the ratio of $X^2$ to the degrees of freedom (df) can serve as a goodness of fit indicator. He cites earlier work by Joreskog and Sorbom (1979) in which the use of the $X^2$/df ratio is recommended as a guide for comparison of the fit of various models in exploratory CFA. The use of a $X^2$/df ratio of 2 as the "cutoff" guide for identifying $X^2$'s which are too large is based on examples and results in Joreskog and Sorbom's 1979 work.

The use of "rules of thumb" as guidelines in assessing CFA models is prevalent throughout the literature which is cited in this study and elsewhere. This practice is due to problems with specific evaluative statistics such as those related to the $X^2$ test discussed above. Rules which have become popular are often based on the results of methodological studies like Joreskog and Sorbom's (1979) or those of Anderson and Gerbing (1984) or Fornell and Larcker (1981). In those studies, various features of the models and tests, such as sample size or level of correlation between variables, are systematically varied to assess the effects of the variation on goodness of fit indicators.

Goodness of fit indicators in addition to $X^2$ are generated by LISREL 7. They are based on differences between the original and reproduced correlation matrices. The Root Mean Square Residual (RMR) is a measure of the average of the "fitted residuals," or differences between the elements of the original and reproduced correlation matrices. The Goodness of Fit Index (GFI) is a ratio of the minimum of the fit function after fitting the model, to the fit function prior to fitting the model. The Adjusted Goodness of Fit Index (AGFI) is the GFI adjusted for the degrees of freedom of the model (Joreskog and Sorbom 1989). Higher values of these ratios indicate a better fit. General guidelines or rules of thumb have been suggested in the literature for using these measures to assess goodness of fit. For example, Bagozzi and Yi (1988) suggest that an AGFI => .9 indicates a good fit. Anderson and Gerbing (1984) point out, however, that variations in sample size will systematically affect the indices, requiring relatively larger values of GFI and AGFI and smaller values of RMR to indicate a good fit as the sample size increases. Finally, assessment of fit is subjective (Bagozzi and Yi 1988) and must be considered in context with regard to individual studies.

Often, analysis of CFA models is performed on a comparative basis, contrasting several proposed models using a single data set. This approach is useful for empirical testing of competing theories in a given research field (Kerlinger 1986). CFA can also be used to examine a data set with regard to competing models which meet a priori expectations of relationships among variables.

In this study, a set of observed measures has been chosen (based both on intuition and past research) to measure credit risk. CFA is then used to investigate the nature of the interrelationships among those variables. When using the scores from CFA to represent the measurement of credit risk in subsequent tests, those scores will represent better measures of credit risk if the associated interrelationships between the original variables are captured. The CFA measurement model is based on the assumption that the better the specified model captures the correlations between the observed variables, the higher the validity of the resulting measure of credit risk. Thus, evidence as to the effectiveness of the measurement - the goodness of fit - is evaluated based on the extent to which the original correlation matrix has been reproduced by the model, both overall and with regard to individual variables. In this study, the three-factor model described above is compared with a one-factor model, which assumes that all seven of the variables contribute to one general measure of credit risk. Subsequently, the three-factor model is expanded into a hierarchical model, which assumes that its three latent variables comprise an intermediate measure of a second-order factor, CRISK.

Statistical testing for differences between comparative models is accomplished using the $X^2$ difference test. The $X^2$ difference test can be used with both ML and GLS estimation to test for differences in the parameters between two models which are nested. Models are said to be nested when one model has more constraints specified and thus is a specialized version of the other (Bentler and Bonett 1980, Bentler and Chou 1987, Long 1983, Loehlin, 1987). The one-factor and three-factor models are nested since the one-factor model can be obtained by constraining the correlations between the latent variables in the three-factor model to a value of one. Since this indicates perfect correlation between the three factors, they are then the equivalent of the one general factor in the one-factor model. Results of $X^2$ difference tests between the one and three-factor models are supplemented with other goodness-of-fit measures.

The test involves taking the difference between the values of $X^2$ computed for the two models (the $X^2$ variate) and, using the difference between the degrees of freedom for the two models as the number of degrees of freedom for the difference test, evaluating the $X^2$ variate against a critical value in the $X^2$ distribution. The hypothesis tested is that the two models are significantly different vis a vis the null hypothesis of model equivalence. Other indicators of model fit noted above also confirm that the statistical difference between the models (due to the additional constraints) indicates an improvement in fit. In the case of nested models, the difference can only represent an improvement in fit from a restricted model to a model with fewer restrictions, since a restriction added to a specific model makes it more difficult to reproduce the original correlation matrix (Long 1983, Marsh 1985). The goodness-of-fit for a hierarchical model, then, can be assessed by the closeness with which it approaches the fit of the three-factor model. Similarly, the fit of the three-factor model can be assessed by the improvements realized when correlations between latent variables are estimated, rather than being restricted to values of one as in the one-factor model.

*Goodness of Fit: One-Factor and Three-Factor Models*

The results of both ML and GLS estimation of the one-factor and three-factor models are presented in Figure 4. The more restricted one-factor model serves as a baseline model[54] and is compared with the three-factor model using a $X^2$ difference test. The difference test indicates a significant difference between the one-factor and the three-factor versions of the models using either ML or GLS. Increases in the goodness of fit indices, GFI and AGFI, and the reduction in the RMR indicate that the three-factor model represents an improvement over the one-factor model, since it reproduces the original correlation matrix more closely.

The initial solution for the three-factor ML model (not reported in Figure 4) included a negative estimated variance for the unique error associated with STDEV. This form of anomaly (an improper solution) occurs in CFA with relative frequency, particularly in studies using small samples (e.g. less than 150; Anderson and Gerbing 1984). In such cases, Bagozzi and Yi (1988) suggest reestimating the model after fixing the offending variance to a very small positive number. The resulting solution can then be compared with the original to insure the parameters have not been significantly changed by the corrective measure. In this case, the variance for

*Analysis and Interpretation of Research Results* 77

STDEV was fixed to .001, and the change in the model ($X^2 = 0.42$ with 1 degree of freedom) was not significant at p=0.05. Thus, the modified three-factor ML model was accepted as a substitute for the original improper solution. The results using the modification are reported in Figure 4.

| Figure 4 | | RESULTS OF ESTIMATION: 1-FACTOR AND 3-FACTOR MODELS | | | | | |
|---|---|---|---|---|---|---|---|
| | | generalized least squares maximum likelihood | | | | | |
| | $X^2$ | DF | $X^2/df$ | GFI | AGFI | RMR | |
| 1 FACTOR | 56.11 | 14 | 4.01 | .841 | .683 | .222 | |
| | 121.14 | 14 | 8.65 | .741 | .482 | .158 | |
| 3 FACTOR | 21.47 | 11 | 1.95 | .939 | .845 | .083 | |
| | 30.00 | 12[55] | 2.50 | .920 | .814 | .063 | |
| $X^2$ difference test: | | | GLS | | ML | | |
| $X^2$ variate | | | 36.64 | | 91.14 | | |
| df | | | 3 | | 2 | | |
| significant at p = | | | .000 | | .000 | | |

Using either the ML or GLS fitting functions, the three-factor model exhibits a good overall fit. Although the formal $X^2$ test would indicate rejection of all models (p=0.000), when used instead as a goodness-of-fit indicator, the ratio of $X^2$ to degrees of freedom is close to 2 for both sets of three-factor estimates. The GFI and AGFI are reasonably high, exceeding .9 and .8 respectively. Although the AGFI values do not exceed Bagozzi and Yi's rule of thumb of .90 mentioned above, a measurement model sample size of 102 is relatively small, resulting in lower expected GFI and AGFI values (Anderson and Gerbing 1984). Also, the GFI and AGFI are high with regard to the baseline, one-factor model. The RMR is quite low using either ML or

GLS, and dramatically lower than the RMR values obtained from the one-factor model.

Standardized residuals[56] are also reported and should be relatively small. Bagozzi and Yi (1988) point out that (absolute) values greater than 2 are indicators of significant amounts of unexplained variance, and thus perhaps also of model specification error. The standardized residuals resulting from the three-factor CFA runs are shown in Figure 5. Ten of the fifty-six standardized residuals (6 for GLS and 4 for ML) exceed 2, which may indicate weakness of fit or poor model specification, but the remaining forty-six residuals are small.

| Figure 5 | | | STANDARDIZED RESIDUALS: GLS/ML | | | | |
|---|---|---|---|---|---|---|---|
| | DRAT | LN ASSET | EXC | DIV | NOSH | STDEV | BETA |
| DRAT | .605 .000 | | | | | | |
| LN ASSET | -.752 -.611 | 8.125 0.000 | | | | | |
| EXC | 0.830 1.380 | -2.094 -1.186 | 1.338 0.000 | | | | |
| DIV | .840 .000 | -.868 -.678 | 1.544 2.113 | 1.297 -.241 | | | |
| NOSH | -.939 -.651 | 1.681 3.607 | -2.781 -2.153 | -.567 -.241 | 2.337 0.000 | | |
| STDEV | -.027 -.268 | -.046 .068 | .270 .212 | .508 .268 | -.281 -.264 | .037 .000 | |
| BETA | 1.370 0.879 | -.316 -.306 | .941 .903 | -.267 -.417 | -2.623 -2.716 | .366 .000 | 2.033 0.000 |

*Evaluation of Individual Variables: Three Factor Model*

CFA models can also be evaluated by looking at indicators related to specific variables, either observed or latent. For example, coefficient estimates (the loadings of observed variables on the latent variables) should generally be large. Bagozzi and Yi (1988) recommend loadings of between .5 and .95 for good models. T-tests of the null hypothesis that each coefficient is zero are used to test the significance of variables. Since the t-test is two-tailed with (N-2) degrees of freedom, values of t close to 2 indicate significance of the coefficients at $p=0.05$ for most sample sizes[57]. Coefficients, their standard errors, and their associated t-statistics are shown in Figure 6. All are significant at less than $p=0.05$.

| Figure 6 | PARAMETER COEFFICIENTS (Standard Errors) | | |
|---|---|---|---|
| | | GLS | ML |
| UNIQUE | DRAT | .830 (.084) t=9.936 | .839(.084) t=9.964 |
| | DIV | .869 (.082) t=10.641 | .869(.083) t=10.625 |
| SIZE | LNASSET | .844(.091) t=9.312 | .875(.093) t=9.424 |
| | EXC | .674(.095) t=7.075 | .622(.098) t=6.318 |
| | NOSH | .686(.092) t=7.461 | .685(.097) t=7.079 |
| MKT | STDEV | .971(.098) t=9.912 | 1.00(.070) t=14.198 |
| | BETA | .505(.094) t=5.383 | .502(.093) t=5.400 |

Fornell and Larcker (1981) and Bagozzi and Yi (1988) recommend evaluation of both, (1) the "item" reliability of each observed variable as a measure of a particular latent variable, and (2) composite measures of each construct. For each variable observed, the item reliability represents the proportion of its total variance which is attributable to its relationship with the latent variable it measures. Using the notation introduced above and defining:

$x_i$ = the observed measures (1 to i)

$ksi_j$ = the latent variables (1 to j)

$lambda_{ij}$ = the estimated coefficient for $x_{ij}$ (which is the loading of $x_i$ on $ksi_j$)

theta delta$_i$ = the variance of $x_i$ (which is error variance unrelated to the model)

$$\text{item reliability} = \frac{lambda_{ij}^2}{lambda_{ij}^2 + \text{theta delta}_i}$$

The composite measure of reliability for a latent variable is computed in a similar fashion. It represents that proportion of the variance (of the variables used to measure $ksi_j$) that is related to $ksi_j$, to their combined total variance (including error variance). It is computed as:

$$\text{composite reliability} = \frac{(lambda_{ij})^2}{(lambda_{ij})^2 + \text{theta delta}_{ij}}$$

Another measure that is useful for assessing the validity of a latent variable is the average variance extracted. It represents the amount of variance which is associated with a latent variable in relation to the amount of variance which is due to measurement error (Fornell and Larcker 1981). It is calculated as follows:

$$\text{average variance extracted} = \frac{lambda_{ij}^2}{lambda_{ij}^2 + \text{theta delta}_{ij}}$$

| Figure 7 | RELIABILITY MEASURES: | |
|---|---|---|
| | GLS | ML |
| ITEM RELIABILITIES FOR OBSERVED VARIABLES | | |
| | | |
| DRAT | .704 | .704 |
| LNASSET | .723 | .765 |
| EXC | .497 | .386 |
| DIV | .784 | .770 |
| NOSH | .568 | .469 |
| STDEV | .945 | .999 |
| BETA | .319 | .252 |
| | | |
| COMPOSITE RELIABILITY | | |
| | | |
| UNIQUE | .853 | .849 |
| SIZE | .817 | .775 |
| MKT | .784 | .751 |
| | | |
| AVERAGE VARIANCE EXTRACTED | | |
| | | |
| UNIQUE | .744 | .737 |
| SIZE | .601 | .755 |
| MKT | .667 | .626 |

The average variance extracted can also be used to evaluate discriminant validity (Fornell and Larcker 1981), that is, the effectiveness with which the measurement model discriminates between two latent variables. Discriminant validity of the latent variables is assessed by comparing the average variance extracted with the squared correlations between pairs of constructs. The average variance extracted should be greater, demonstrating that the common variation which characterizes each latent variable is greater than that which relates it to the others (Fornell and Larcker 1981). The entries in the matrix in Figure 8 are the squared correlations between the latent variables. All meet the criteria for discriminant validity.

Computed values for the item reliability of each observed variable, as well as the composite reliability and variance extracted for each latent variable based on estimations of the three-factor model are shown in Figure 7. Bagozzi and Yi (1988) suggest that item reliability should equal or exceed .5 and composite reliability should equal or exceed .6 in model evaluation. They also suggest that the average variance extracted exceed .5, as do Fornell and Larcker (1981), since when this is not the case, the variance due to measurement error is greater than the amount of variance captured by the latent variable. As shown below, EXC, BETA and NOSH exhibit weak item reliability using .5 as a benchmark. All of the measures of composite reliability, however, exceed .6, and the average variance extracted exceeds .5 in each case.    These indicators provide additional evidence of a reasonably good fit for the three-factor credit risk measurement model.

| Figure 8 | INDICATORS OF DISCRIMINANT VALIDITY | | |
|---|---|---|---|
| Squared Correlations Between Latent Variables | | | |
| | UNIQUE | SIZE | MKT |
| SIZE | .308 GLS .268 ML | | |
| MKT | .610 GLS .555 ML | .005 GLS .005 ML | |
| Average Variance Extracted | | | |
| GLS | .744 | .601 | .667 |
| ML | .737 | .755 | .626 |

*Hierarchical Factor Analysis*

Having established that the goodness of fit of the three-factor credit risk model is acceptable and also that it provides a better fit than the one-factor model,  one latent variable model remains to be tested. This is a hierarchical, or second-order, model.   It is based on the assumption that there is a second-order latent variable CRISK characterized by the correlations between the first-order latent variables UNIQUE, SIZE, AND MKT. LISREL 7 was also used to test this model. Generally, the identification of a second order latent variable provides evidence that the three first order variables do represent a single, measurable construct. The alternative interpretation would be that the three factors are correlated but largely independent features of the firm. In this case, their traditional association with the credit risk of the firm provides support for characterizing their relationship. Given a satisfactory fit, the hierarchical model could be accepted as a parsimonious substitute for the three-factor model based on a non-significant $X^2$ difference test. In that case, only one latent variable (one set of factor scores) would suffice to represent credit risk in subsequent analysis. This second-order latent variable would differ from the one-factor representation of the model which was evaluated earlier, by its second-order status. That is, CRISK would represent a factor for which the immediate measurement source was the correlation between latent variables. It would represent a single, but multidimensional, construct, rather than the unidimensional construct which results from a one factor model. Specifically, CRISK would represent a single, but multidimensional, second-order latent variable which could be measured using the underlying latent variables MKT, UNIQUE, and SIZE.

The discussion of second-order analysis is limited to ML estimation, because convergence was not achieved using GLS. This was the first indication that the second-order model was unsatisfactory. Using ML estimation, two negative variance estimates were produced. As mentioned earlier, this type of anomoly is not unusual in the estimation of CFA models, but represents an improper solution. If the model parameters change significantly when it is reestimated after fixing the offending variance to a small positive number, then the negative variance indicates problems such as specification errors, or violations of underlying assumptions of the model, and the fit questionable (Bagozzi and Yi 1988, Anderson and Gerbing 1984). After constraining the variance associated with STDEV to .001 as was done with the three-factor model above, the change was insignificant at p=0.05 ($X^2 = .42$, 1 df). However, when a negative estimate for the variance of UNIQUE was also set to .001, the change was significant ($X^2 = 18.86$, 2 df). Since the second-order solution did not provide a good fit given the current data, the three-factor model, which did fit the data reasonably well, was accepted as a representation of credit risk for further use in this study. Factor scores were developed using the regression coefficients[58] from this model (Figure 9). These scores represent correlated measures of UNIQUE, SIZE, and MKT, and serve as independent variables in the multinomial logit model.

| FIGURE 9 | COEFFICIENTS FOR CALCULATION OF FACTOR SCORES: | | |
|---|---|---|---|
| | GLS (ML) | | |
| | UNIQUE | SIZE | MKT |
| DRAT | .268(.298) | .108(.091) | -.051(-.001) |
| LNASSET | .116(.120) | .464(.589) | .026(.000) |
| EXC | .055(.033) | .220(.160) | .012(.000) |
| DIV | .388(.402) | .156(.123) | -.074(-.001) |
| NOSH | .016(.000) | .287(.204) | .016(.000) |
| STDEV | -.314(-.285) | .149(.120) | .872(.998) |
| BETA | -.017(.000) | .008(.000) | .046(.001) |

## MULTINOMIAL LOGIT ANALYSIS

*Method of Analysis*

The multinomial logit model in this study is estimated using the *LOGIT* module of *SYSTAT* (Steinberg 1988). The model provides the basis for estimating the probability that a firm will disclose at a particular level of DSCQ given their set of associated attributes. It also serves to identify the independent variables in the model which are significant predictors of that outcome.

Multinomial logit analysis can be described briefly as follows. For each firm i a set of disclosure attributes and a set of k independent (credit risk and ownership structure) variables $X_k$ is observed. The disclosure attributes are summed and collapsed into three categories of DSCQ as follows:

DSCQ = 1     if less than 5 attributes were observed,

DSCQ = 2     if  5  attributes  were  observed,

DSCQ = 3     if  more  than  5  attributes  were observed.

Using the observed probability of having disclosed at a given level of DSCQ and the set of $X_k$ disclosure attributes for each firm i, a set of maximimum likelihood coefficients for the credit risk and ownership attributes at the first 2 of the 3 levels of DSCQ in the study is estimated[59]. This set of estimated coefficients can then be used to estimate the probability ($P_{ij}$) that firm i will disclose at level $DSCQ_j$.

Let $z_{ij} = \text{constant} + B_{j1}X_{i1} + B_{j2}X_{i2} + ... + B_{jk}X_{ik}$, where $B_{jk}$ is the estimated coefficient for variable k and DSCQ level j, and $X_{ik}$ is the observed value for variable k and firm i. The predicted probability of observing a given disclosure level for each firm can then be computed using the following expression:

$$P_{ij} = \frac{e^{z_{ij}}}{\sum_{j=1}^{J} e^{z_{ij}}}$$

The overall fit of the model can be evaluated by comparing the fit between the calculated probabilities and the observed responses. A $X^2$ statistic is used to test the hypothesis that all coefficients except the constant are equal to zero. Individual t-tests of the coefficients are used to test the significance of the independent variables ($H_0$: $B_k = 0$). The application of multinomial logit analysis to the models in the study, and an analysis of the related findings are described below.

*The Full Model*

After the credit risk variables (UNIQUE, SIZE, and MKT) were determined using CFA, the specification of the multinomial logit model described in Chapter 3 required modification. This is because the number of shareholders (NOSH) was used in the CFA model as an observed measure of SIZE. The multinomial logit model, which includes the variable NOSH indirectly through the latent variable SIZE, is shown in Figure 10.

| Figure 10 | MULTINOMIAL LOGIT ANALYSIS: THE FULL MODEL | | | |
|---|---|---|---|---|
| PROB [DSCQ] $=a + b_1$ MGR $+ b_2$ MGR$^2$ $+ b_3$ OC$+$ $b_4$ UNIQUE$+ b_5$ SIZE $+ b_6$ MKT | | | | |
| | coefficient | | | |
| | GLS | | (t-value) | ML |
| | P(DSCQ)=1 | P(DSCQ)=2 | P(DSCQ)=1 | P(DSCQ)=2 |
| CONSTANT | -1.5466 | -4.2718 | -1.6626 | -4.3315 |
| | (-0.423) | (-1.007) | (-0.438) | (-0.983) |
| MGR | 0.00697 | 0.1758 | 0.00703 | 0.1763 |
| | (0.1453) | (2.158) | (0.1466) | (2.162) |
| MGR$^2$ | -.00009 | -0.0032 | -.00009 | -0.0032 |
| | (-0.141) | (-1.857) | (-0.142) | (-1.863) |
| OC | 0.6511 | -0.2078 | 0.6515 | -0.2073 |
| | (1.172) | (-0.274) | (1.172) | (-.0273) |
| UNIQUE | -0.5969 | 0.0764 | -0.4134 | 0.2222 |
| | (-0.329) | (0.034) | (-0.310) | (0.132) |
| SIZE | 0.1805 | 0.0145 | 0.0831 | -0.0446 |
| | (0.338) | (0.022) | (0.310) | (-0.131) |
| MKT | -0.5505 | -0.6040 | -0.4155 | -0.4827 |
| | (-0.352) | (-0.322) | (-0.360) | (-0.351) |
| $X^2$ (df) | 10.467(12) | | 10.463(12) | |

The parameter estimates and associated t-values from multinomial logit analysis are also shown in Figure 10. Two versions of the model were estimated, incorporating credit risk variables (scores) developed alternatively from ML or GLS estimation of the three-factor CFA model. The results are similar for the ML and GLS estimations. The overall $X^2$ test was not significant at conventional levels for either model. The only variable for which the individual coefficient is significant at p=0.05 is MGR. Since the coefficients for all of the credit risk variables developed using CFA are insignificant, *the hypothesis that disclosure quality is significantly related to the credit risk of firms using interest rate swaps is not confirmed by multinomial logit analysis.* There are a number of potential explanations for the nonsignificance of the credit risk variables in this study. In addition to the obvious inference that no significant relationship exists, current features of swap disclosure and the design of the tests in this study may have combined to produce this outcome despite the existence of an underlying relationship between disclosure quality and credit risk. These potential confounds and alternative explanations are discussed in Chapter 5.

The failure of the multinomial logit analysis to confirm an association between disclosure quality and credit riskiness among swap-users does not, however, preclude the possibility of significant findings with regard to ownership structure. In order to narrow the research focus to tests of association between disclosure quality and ownership structure, the model was revised to eliminate the latent variables representing credit risk, and to include those variables assumed to be associated with ownership structure, MGR, OC, and NOSH, as described in Chapter 3.

As discussed earlier, tests of hypotheses related to ownership structure generally include some of the same variables which are associated with credit risk, particularly indicators of firm size and leverage. Accordingly, LNASSET and DE have been included as control variables as indicators of these two elements, respectively. This model was estimated using the original data set of 102 firms. In addition, sufficient data was available to estimate this revised model for an additional 63 swap-disclosing firms, resulting in a pooled data set of 165 firms.

Results for both the original 102 firms, as well as the full set of 165 are reported in Figure 11. The overall $X^2$ statistics were not significant (at p=0.05), but individual coefficients for MGR, $MGR^2$ and LNASSET were significant for the 102 firm sample. The estimated coefficient for NOSH was insignificant and also very small (0.000001 at P(DSCQ=1), -0.000004 at P(DSCQ=2), N=102). Since its coefficient was very close to zero, NOSH was removed from the model. The model was then estimated again, this time for 63, 102 and

165, but without NOSH. The resulting estimates (Figure 12) are similar to the initial estimates, but the reduction in degrees of freedom makes the overall $X^2$ estimate significant at a level between p=0.10 and p=0.05 when N=102. The similarities in results between the models in Figures 11 and 12 include non-significant coefficients both for OC and DE. A version of the model which includes only the managerial ownership and size variables (Figure 13) was also estimated and found to be significant ($X^2 = 14.5446$, p < 0.05) when N=102.

| Figure 11 | INITIAL OWNERSHIP STRUCTURE MODEL | | |
|---|---|---|---|
| PROB [DSCQ] = $a + b_1$ MGR + $b_2$ MGR$^2$ + $b_3$ OC + $b_4$ NOSH + $b_5$ LNASSET + $b_6$ DE | | | |
| | coefficient | | |
| | N=102 (t-value) | | N=165 |
| | P(DSCQ)=1 | P(DSCQ)=2 | P(DSCQ)=1 | P(DSCQ)=2 |
| CONSTANT | -2.1848 | -7.4130 | -1.9395 | -1.5763 |
| | (-0.886) | (-2.070) | (-1.468) | (-1.114) |
| MGR | 0.0367 | 0.2601 | 0.01799 | 0.0283 |
| | (0.702) | (2.762) | (0.568) | (0.821) |
| MGR$^2$ | -0.0004 | -0.0046 | -0.0003 | -0.0004 |
| | (-0.585) | (-2.385) | (-0.743) | (-1.020) |
| OC | 0.7654 | -0.0576 | 0.1591 | 0.0990 |
| | (1.334) | (-0.074) | (0.361) | (0.198) |
| NOSH | 0.000001 | -0.000003 | -0.000001 | -0.00001 |
| | (0.107) | (-0.338) | (-0.239) | (-0.714) |
| LNASSET | 0.3897 | 0.8086 | 0.2300 | 0.1314 |
| | (1.642) | | (2.478) | |
| DE | -0.0161 | -0.0019 | -0.0291 | -0.0124 |
| | (-0.574) | (-0.045) | (-1.127) | (-0.446) |
| $X^2$(df) | 17.480(12) | | 7.169(12) | |

The results of the model described in Figure 12 serve as the focus for the remainder of the analysis. Although the overall $X^2$ for the model is only marginally significant,[60] a specification of the model without the OC and DE variables would be inconsistent with findings in past studies of ownership structure in which DE has been included as a control variable, and OC is a primary measure of owner control (e.g. Dhaliwal, *et al* 1982).

| Figure 12 | REVISED OWNERSHIP STRUCTURE MODEL | | | | |
|---|---|---|---|---|---|
| PROB [DSCQ] = a + $b_1$ MGR + $b_2$ MGR$^2$ + $b_3$ OC + $b_4$ LNASSET + $b_5$ DE | | | | | |
| | coefficient (t-value) | | | | |
| | N=102 P(DSCQ)= | | N=165 P(DSCQ)= | | N=63 P(DSCQ)= |
| | 1 | 2 | 1 | 2 | 1 | 2 |
| CONSTANT | -2.2753 (-0.965) | -7.0813 (-2.052) | -1.8332 (-1.522) | -1.1849 (-0.905) | -0.3319 (-0.156) | 4.7085 (1.917) |
| MGR | 0.0364 (0.696) | 0.2626 (2.789) | 0.01759 (0.558) | 0.0282 (0.813) | 0.9922 (0.204) | -0.9997 (-1.770) |
| MGR$^2$ | -0.0004 (-0.577) | -0.0047 (-2.406) | -0.0003 (-0.732) | -0.0004 (-1.007) | -0.0002 (-0.301) | 0.0010 (1.589) |
| OC | 0.7594 (1.327) | -0.0630 (-0.080) | 0.1634 (0.371) | 0.1249 (0.251) | -0.6117 (-0.699) | -0.2212 (-0.240) |
| LNASSET | 0.4050 (2.017) | 0.7497 (2.683) | 0.2107 (1.450) | 0.0570 (0.356) | 0.2450 (0.106) | -0.6037 (-2.085) |
| DE | -0.0160 (-0.570) | -0.0020 (-0.046) | -0.0291 (-1.128) | -0.0126 (-0.454) | -0.4298 (-0.638) | -0.1134 (-0.996) |
| $X^2$ (df) | 17.262 (10) | | 6.591 (10) | | 10.151 (10) | |

An important feature of the multinomial logit results is that coefficient estimates are significant only for the sample of 102. This implies that the additional set of 63 firms differs from the original 102 firms in ways which are related to the variables in the models. Tests of differences between the means of variables in the 102 and 63 firm groups (Figure 14) indicate significant differences for all of the variables except DE and NOSH. In particular, the mean percentage of shares owned by managers and directors is higher in the 63 firm group. That difference is important because the anticipated nonlinearity in the relationship between DSCQ and MGR (which is dependent on the dominance of either the alignment or entrenchment effect) may occur at a particular level of MGR. If this is the case, then the addition of firms having predominantly higher levels of MGR would make that effect more difficult to detect in the pooled sample of 165.

| Figure 13 | | | | | | |
|---|---|---|---|---|---|---|
| ABBREVIATED OWNERSHIP STRUCTURE MODEL | | | | | | |
| PROB [DSCQ] = a + $b_1$ MGR + $b_2$ MGR$^2$ + $b_3$ LNASSET | | | | | | |
| | | coefficient (t-value) | | | | |
| | N=102 | | N=165 | | N=63 | |
| | P(DSCQ)= | | P(DSCQ)= | | P(DSCQ)= | |
| | 1 | 2 | 1 | 2 | 1 | 2 |
| CONSTANT | -2.7237 | -7.0754 | -1.6137 | -1.0822 | -0.9221 | 4.0129 |
| | (-1.768) | (-3.080) | (-1.390) | (-0.849) | (-0.471) | (1.848) |
| MGR | 0.0583 | 0.2515 | 0.02238 | 0.0321 | 0.0107 | -0.0789 |
| | (1.194) | (2.981) | (0.761) | (0.995) | (0.237) | (-1.553) |
| MGR$^2$ | -0.0006 | -0.0045 | -0.0003 | -0.0005 | -0.0002 | 0.0007 |
| | (-0.911) | (-2.410) | (-0.983) | (-1.192) | (-0.473) | (1.258) |
| LNASSET | 0.3431 | 0.7370 | 0.1843 | 0.0460 | 0.3768 | -0.5713 |
| | (1.776) | (2.706) | (1.293) | (0.290) | (0.166) | (-2.069) |
| $X^2$ (df) | 14.545 (6) | | 4.894 (6) | | 7.283 (6) | |

Evidence which supports the assumption of homogeneity of the groups and the use of the pooled sample is provided by a Chow test.[61] The results of the Chow test allow acceptance of the hypothesis that coefficients from OLS regressions using the samples of 63 and 102 are the same at p=0.05.

| Figure | DESCRIPTIVE STATISTICS | | |
| --- | --- | --- | --- |
| | | mean | |
| | | standard deviation | |
| N = | 102 | 63 | 165 |
| | | | |
| DSCQ | 1.980 | 2.270 | 2.091 |
| | 0.890 | 0.827 | 0.875 |
| | | | |
| MGR | 8.993 | 27.969 | 16.239 |
| | 15.228 | 30.705 | 24.182 |
| | | | |
| OC | 0.431 | 0.810 | 0.576 |
| | 0.498 | 0.396 | 0.496 |
| | | | |
| LNASSET | 7.263 | 6.640 | 7.025 |
| | 1.417 | 1.772 | 1.586 |
| | | | |
| DE | 0.771 | 3.418 | 1.782 |
| | 8.094 | 10.643 | 9.210 |

| Tests of $H_0$: the means are equal in N=102 and N=63: | | |
| --- | --- | --- |
| | t | p |
| DSCQ | 2.121 | 0.036 |
| MGR | 4.570 | 0.000 |
| LNASSET | 2.360 | 0.020 |
| OC | 5.394 | 0.000 |
| DE | 1.695 | 0.093 |
| NOSH | 0.690 | 0.493 |

The insignificance of the multinomial logit results for the 165 firm sample indicates that the expected relationships between variables either are not present in the data, or are present to an extent or in a form which is not detectable using multinomial logit analysis. If the relationships are similar, but simply less pronounced after the addition of 63 firms, then differences between the groups could have interesting implications with regard to disclosure.[62] The following analysis is designed to contrast the group of 63 to the original 102 firms, and also to point out similarities and reasons for differences between the original and pooled samples. The goal is to provide insight as to why anticipated relationships are significant only in the original sample.

*Comparative Analysis of Ownership Structure Models*

A comparison of the original and pooled data sets is important in this study because the original set of 102 firms is the group for which the model yields significant results. These results confirm relationships which have regulatory implications for swap disclosure which, if applied in a regulatory setting, are likely to affect the entire population of firms which engage in swaps. If there is reason to believe the results in the original group also apply to the pooled sample, or that systematic differences in the group of 63 render different implications for swap disclosure, these reasons are important from a regulatory perspective.

There are a number of similarities between the functions implied by multinomial analysis in the three data sets and in the relationships between independent variables implicit in those functions. For example, the signs of all of the estimated coefficients are the same for both the original and pooled samples, with the exception of OC at $P(DSCQ=2)$. The coefficient estimate for OC, however, is not significant in either group (See Figure 12). Interestingly, in the set of 63 firms, the signs of the coefficients for the MGR, $MGR^2$, and LNASSET variables are opposite of those in the other two groups for $P(DSCQ=2)$. This is consistent with the higher overall level of DSCQ in the group of 63 (i.e. in this group, the midlevel is more like the high than the low disclosure quality level) and it serves to reduce the significance of the findings in the pooled sample.

*Predictive accuracy of the models*

The probability of observing either of the first two levels of DSCQ for an individual firm is estimated by applying the appropriate set of coefficients from the model to the observed data values for that firm. Then $P(DSCQ=3)$ is found by subtracting the sum of the first two probabilities from 1. Using the DSCQ level with the highest probability of being chosen as the predicted disclosure level for each firm, that prediction can be compared with the observed DSCQ. The percentage of correct predictions then serves as a measure of effectiveness for the models. The percentage of correct predictions for both the original and pooled models [48% (49 of 102) and 45.5% (75 of 165)] is higher than the 33.3% rate which would be expected based only on chance. They are not particularly encouraging, however, since fewer than half of the predictions are correct for each model. Predictions based on mean values of the independent variables can also be used as summary measures of the predictive accuracy of the models. These measures present the models in a more favorable light. Since the objective of this study is to examine general relationships between the quality of disclosure and the independent variables, as opposed to developing a model to predict the activity of an individual firm, this measure is also more appropriate. As shown in Figure 15, the 165 firm model is a more successful predictor than the 102 or 63 firm models using this criterion.

| Figure 15 | PREDICTIVE ACCURACY OF THE MODEL | | |
|---|---|---|---|
| | DSCQ | OBSERVED | PREDICTED |
| N=102 | 1 | .402 | .439 |
| | 2 | .216 | .163 |
| | 3 | .382 | .398 |
| N=63 | 1 | .238 | .246 |
| | 2 | .254 | .201 |
| | 3 | .508 | .554 |
| N=165 | 1 | .339 | .336 |
| | 2 | .230 | .231 |
| | 3 | .430 | .432 |

*Changes in the Probability of High Quality Disclosure*

In multinomial logit analysis, the sign of a coefficient is not a consistent indicator of the direction of change in corresponding probabilities. This limits prediction of directional changes (such as in the probability of observing high quality disclosure) to relative changes between a single pair of alternatives. For example, the difference between the coefficients (Figure 12) for MGR (N=102) at P(DSCQ=1) and P(DSCQ=2) is:

$$0.0364 - 0.2626 = -0.2262$$

Since this difference is negative, the model implies that increases in MGR will decrease the likelihood of observing DSCQ=1 relative to DSCQ=2. However, both probabilities may increase with an increase in MGR, as long as P(DSCQ=2) increases less than P(DSCQ=1). Concurrent changes, such as the effect of increases in MGR on P(DSCQ=3), must be considered separately (Aldrich and Nelson 1984). Clearly, the use of the signs of coefficients in the analysis of multinomial logit models is unwieldy and, in this study, not particularly informative.

When comparing the models, information on the changes they imply in individual probabilities (e.g. the probability of observing high quality disclosure, or P(DSCQ)=3) at selected values of the variables is more informative. For instance, given a particular size firm and levels of DE and OC, it is possible to graph the changes in P(DSCQ)=3 which would occur as MGR increases, as implied by the current model. The model coefficients were used to compute the estimated probabilities P(DSCQ=1) and P(DSCQ=2) as described earlier, with P(DSCQ=3) equal to 1 - [P(DSCQ=1) + P(DSCQ=2)]. In graphs presented in Appendix D, estimated coefficients are applied to fixed values for all independent variables except one, the behavior of which is then presented graphically with regard to changes in the probability of observing DSCQ=3 for N=102 and N=165, or DSCQ=(2 or 3) in the case of N=63.

In addition to presenting the data relationships implied by the models, actual observations of the most highly significant variables were also investigated in greater depth. Subsamples of the original and pooled data sets were created by dividing them on the basis of either MGR or LNASSET.[63] The subsamples were then compared using nonparametric tests within and between the two data sets. The results of these tests tend to support the original hypotheses, as well as the relationships implied by the multinomial logit models. They are described in the following sections.

*Levels of Managerial Ownership*

As shown in Figure 16, both samples were divided into thirds on the basis of MGR. Mann-Whitney U tests for a decrease in DSCQ between the low and mid-levels of MGR, and an increase in DSCQ between the mid-level and highest level of MGR, confirm most of the expected relationships. The expected decrease between the low and mid-levels is significant for 102 firms (p=0.041) but not for 165 firms. In a second test of the 165 firm sample, the levels were adjusted to match the ranges of MGR which occurred in the evenly divided 102 firm sample. This change made the test more comparable between groups and also rendered more highly significant results for the difference between the low and mid-levels. The tests provide additional evidence of the anticipated non-linear relationship between MGR and DSCQ in both data sets.

| Figure 16 | | DSCQ OVER LEVELS OF MGR MANN-WHITNEY U TESTS: | | |
|---|---|---|---|---|
| | | $H_0$: | $MGR_1 > MGR_2$ | $MGR_2 < MGR_3$ |
| N=102: | | | | |
| $MGR_1$ | 0.00 - 1.35% $n_1 = 34$ | U | 436.5 | 694 |
| $MGR_2$ | 1.40 - 5.60% $n_2 = 34$ | z | -1.74 | 1.42 |
| $MGR_3$ | => 5.96% $n_3 = 34$ | p | .041 | .078 |
| N=165: | | | | |
| $MGR_1$ | 0.00 - 1.50% $n_1 = 55$ | U | 1473 | 1754 |
| $MGR_2$ | 1.60 - 11.1% $n_2 = 55$ | z | -0.24 | 1.44 |
| $MGR_3$ | 11.2 - 98.5% $n_3 = 55$ | p | .405 | .075 |
| N=165: | | | | |
| $MGR_1$ | 0.00 - 1.35% $n_1 = 49$ | U | 807.5 | 1795 |
| $MGR_2$ | 1.40 - 5.60% $n_2 = 39$ | z | -1.24 | 1.72 |
| $MGR_3$ | => 5.96% $n_3 = 77$ | p | .108 | .044 |

Prior studies have not established precise ranges of management ownership over which the entrenchment effect might be expected to dominate (or give way to) the alignment effect. When Morck *et al* (1988) proposed the relationship which is investigated here, its form was based on the results of their descriptive data analysis. Framed in terms of the variables in this study, their results would cause one to expect a positive relationship with DSCQ from the 0 to 5% range of MGR, a negative relationship from the 5% to the 25% range, and a positive relationship for MGR => 25%. This implies a cubic relationship between the two variables.[64] The results from Morck *et al* (1988) are not directly comparable to the variables in this study, however, since they used a measure of board ownership rather than MGR, and a different dependent variable (Tobin's Q).

Subsequent related studies used measures for managerial ownership more comparable to MGR. The form of the hypothesized relationships varied, however. Niehaus' (1989) hypothesis was structured as a quadratic function, while Francis and Wilson (1988) adopted the levels suggested by Morck *et al* (1988), but used a dichotomous variable set to 1 if the ownership level was within the ranges in which positive change was expected. Niehaus' (1989) formulation was significant in empirical tests; Francis and Wilson's (1988) was not.

Niehaus (1989) presented the frequencies with which firms in his sample were observed to use LIFO (beneficial to shareholders) rather than FIFO (beneficial to managers) over levels of managerial ownership. His data indicates a decreasing use of LIFO over all ranges up to the 26.3% level of ownership, and increasing use above that level, which can be interpreted as evidence that managerial discretion (entrenchment) is low when ownership is at or near zero and increases with ownership up to the 26.3% level, but thereafter is offset by the alignment effect. The results of the multinomial logit analysis in this study are also consistent with Niehaus's implication. They exhibit a decline in P(DSCQ)=3 over the range of MGR from 0 to approximately 30%[65] and an increase thereafter.

The implied relationships are evident when the results of the multinomial logit analysis are examined graphically. In the graphs below, the Y axis represents the probability of observing high disclosure quality, P(DSCQ=3) for N=102 or 165, or P(DSCQ=2 or 3) for N=63, computed using the coefficients from the multinomial logit analyses. The values for other independent variables in the model were held constant (as shown at the top of the graphs), while the values for MGR were allowed to vary from 0 to 100%. Inspection of these graphs indicates, although less obviously when N=165, that the estimated probability of observing high quality disclosure declines over the low range of MGR and increases beginning from approximately 30%.

A potential explanation for the difference in the 165 firm group is the increase in the number of firms having high managerial ownership. High MGR is likely to be related to the reasons the 63 firms were not included in the original tests. Of the 63, 54 were not included because they did not have published betas (generally because they had not been traded for a sufficient period) or because CRSP returns were not available.[66] Data from the CRSP Over The Counter tape was not available for this study, so OTC firms are disproportionately represented in the group of 63. Firms for which betas are not published, because data about their performance has only been available for a short period of time, for example, might be expected to be smaller and have higher levels of MGR, which on average is the case.

The Niehaus (1989) and Morck *et al* (1988) studies, on the other hand, included only Fortune 500 firms, most of which are large and traded on the New York Stock Exchange. Only 5% of the 344 firms in the Niehaus (1989) study have managerial ownership in excess of 26.3%. In Morck *et al* (1988), 11.6% of the 371 firms in the study have ownership exceeding 30%. This differs from the 165 firm sample which has MGR in excess of 30% for 19.4%, or 32 of 165 firms. The 102 firm sample is most similar to Niehaus's (1989) with only 7.8% (8 of 102) of the firms having MGR in excess of 30%. It is likely that the differences in the group of 63 firms, particularly in levels of MGR and LNASSET, account for the similarity of results in the group of 102 to results of prior studies, while results of similar tests of 165 firms are insignificant.

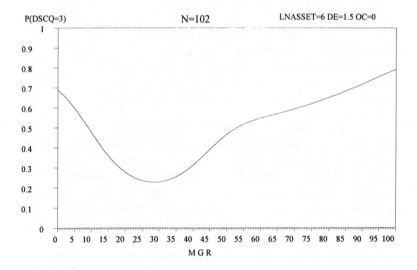

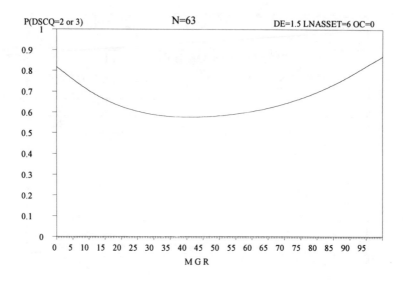

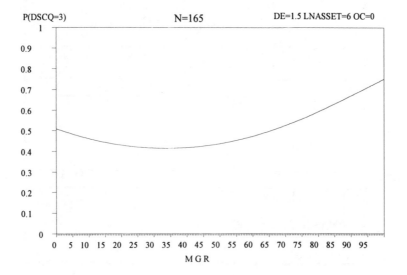

| FIGURE 17 | DSCQ OVER LEVELS OF LNASSET | | | |
|---|---|---|---|---|

JONCKHEERE'S TEST OF ORDERED ALTERNATIVES:
$H_0$: $DSCQ_{LNASSET1} < DSCQ_{LNASSET2} < DSCQ_{LNASSET3}$

| | $n_j$ | J | z | p |
|---|---|---|---|---|
| N=102: | | 1858.5 | 0.76 | 0.224 |
| $LNASSET_1$ 3.733 - 6.648 | 34 | | | |
| $LNASSET_2$ 6.732 - 8.163 | 34 | | | |
| $LNASSET_3$ 8.172 - 10.042 | 34 | | | |
| N=165: | $n_j$ | 5145.5 | 1.82 | 0.034 |
| $LNASSET_1$ 2.596 - 6.213 | 55 | | | |
| $LNASSET_2$ 6.234 - 7.808 | 55 | | | |
| $LNASSET_3$ 7.829 - 11.264 | 55 | | | |

MANN-WHITNEY U TESTS:
$H_0$: $DSCQ_{LNASSETA} < DSCQ_{LNASSETB}$

| | $n_j$ | U | z | p |
|---|---|---|---|---|
| N=102: | | 1517.5 | 1.45 | 0.074 |
| $LNASSET_A$ 3.733 - 7.254 | 51 | | | |
| $LNASSET_B$ 7.275 - 10.042 | 51 | | | |
| N=165: | | 3774 | 1.21 | .113 |
| $LNASSET_A$ 2.596 - 7.020 | 83 | | | |
| $LNASSET_B$ 7.065 - 11.264 | 82 | | | |

*Levels of Firm Size*

Since firm size is an indicator of the dispersion of ownership (i.e. larger firms would generally be expected to be more difficult to monitor and control) the entrenchment effect would be partially offset in the models by adding the 63 firms which are smaller on average than the original 102. In that case mean DSCQ would increase, which is the case here.

In general, however, a declining probability of observing high quality disclosure would be expected as firm size increases, and monitoring of managers becomes more difficult. Jonckheere's test of ordered alternatives, and Mann-Whitney U tests were used to test for anticipated decreases in disclosure quality with increases in firm size. The samples were again stratified by thirds, and also in halves, this time on the basis of LNASSET. The results of these tests were more highly significant for 165 than for 102 firms when stratified by thirds, while the opposite is true when the sample is divided in half (Figure 17).

The changes in P(DSCQ)=3[67] which occur as LNASSET increases[68] as implied by the multinomial logit models are displayed graphically below, with levels of MGR, DE and OC fixed at various representative levels. Clearly, the expected decrease in the probability of observing high disclosure quality as size increases is consistent with the implications of the models estimated using each of the three data sets.

The graphs demonstrate that the implied effects of size and level of managerial ownership on the probability of high quality disclosure are related to one another in the data sets (although again to a greater extent in the original sample) when the graphs of the change in P(DSCQ=3) over the ranges of MGR and LNASSET are compared over the applicable range of values of the fixed variable. Appendix D contains the series of graphs which depict for selected values of LNASSET, the implied probability of high quality disclosure over the range of MGR from 0 to 100%, and for selected values of MGR, the implied P(DSCQ=3)[69] over the ranges of LNASSET found in the two data sets. As the selected values of LNASSET increase, the P(DSCQ=3) decreases over the entire range of MGR. Moreover, the decreasing trend in P(DSCQ=3) over the range of LNASSET is evident as the selected values of MGR increase, but the level of P(DSCQ=3) decreases. The decrease provides evidence of the increasing difficulty of monitoring managers as firms grow, and the increased managerial entrenchment, as well as the lower probability of high quality disclosure of swap transactions which result.

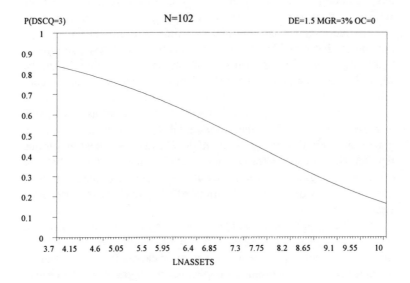

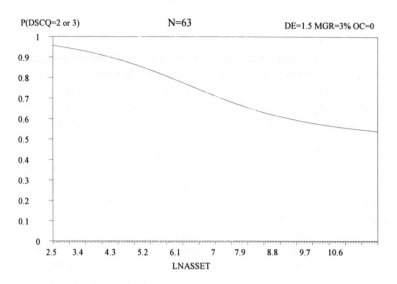

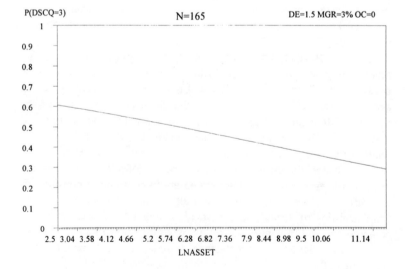

# SUMMARY

The use of Confirmatory Factor Analysis in the identification of a model of credit risk was successful, providing a three-factor model of credit risk to serve as input to subsequent analysis. However, the hypothesized relationship between a firm's credit riskiness and the quality of its swap disclosure was not found to be significant in tests using multinomial logit analysis.

Additional multinomial logit analyses of variables related to ownership structure were conducted. Ownership structure tests were performed using three data sets. One consisted of data for the 102 firms included in earlier analysis. That set was limited by the availability of a complete set of the data items needed for CFA. The second was a data set made up of 63 additional firms for which all data items required in tests of the ownership structure models were available. The third was a pooled sample of the 165 firms from the first two data sets. The test results were significant for the 102 firm data set, but not the others. Since, based on the asymptotic theory which underlies the tests, the statistical significance of relationships between tested variables would be expected to become stronger rather than weaker as the sample size increases, further investigation was warranted.

Results of nonparametric tests of the original and pooled data sets were generally consistent with the hypothesized relationships between DSCQ and both MGR and LNASSET across data sets. In addition, graphical representation of the changes in DSCQ over the ranges of MGR and LNASSET which are implied by the multinomial logit coefficient estimates provide evidence that the expected relationships are present in similar form in all of the data sets.

Systematic differences in the variables of interest between the original 102 firms and the additional 63 are likely to be responsible for the differences in significance in multinomial logit analysis. The characteristics of firms and statistical results in the original group coincide more closely with past studies of ownership structure.

In Chapter 5, conclusions based on these results, and suggestions for related future research are presented.

## Notes

[47] Due to the assumption of CFA that variables are normally distributed, four of the continuous variables were transformed by taking the natural log of the original data items. This transformation produced the changes in distributions for those variables shown below:

| original (transformed) | KURTOSIS | SKEWNESS | STANDARD DEV |
|---|---|---|---|
| CTA | 4.711(.874) | 2.160(-.692) | .068(1.481) |
| DA | 10.686(3.233) | 2.862(1.168) | .249(.290) |
| STDEV | 11.296(1.626) | 2.570(0.378) | .003(.341) |
| LNASSET | 7.895(-.460) | 2.470(-.382) | 3936.7(1.47) |

[48] Total Cash Flow is the sum from the Statement of Cash Flows which includes Net Cash Flow from Operating Activities, from Investing Activities, and from Financing Activities, (Compustat Annual Data Items 308, 311, and 313).

[49] For those firms (28 of 102, 60 of 165) which had no outstanding rated debt, the firms' stock rating was used as a proxy. The classification rule for DRAT was 1 for firms having a stock rating of B+ or higher, 0 otherwise. In general a DRAT of 1 indicates debt to be of investment grade (e.g. a Standard & Poors rating of BBB or higher).

[50] The reader is referred to the cited works for mathematical specification of the polychoric and polyserial correlation coefficients.

[51] The analysis of covariance structures has subsequently been implemented in other available software (e.g. EQS, developed by Peter M. Bentler). They may use different systems of notation. The notation used in LISREL, however, has been widely used in published studies which employ CFA and Covariance Structure Analysis.

[52] This includes 16 factor loadings, 6 latent variable correlations, and 16 measurement error terms. It would require a sample size of 190 to meet Bentler's recommendation.

[53] "The $X^2$ is a valid test statistic only if:

1.        all the observed variables have a multivariate normal distribution,
2.        the analysis is based on the sample covariance matrix
          (standardization is not permitted),
3.        the sample size is fairly large.

All these three assumptions are seldom fulfilled in practice" (Joreskog and Sorbom 1986, I.39)

54 Bentler and Bonett (1980) recommend comparison of the model to be tested with a "null" model - or saturated model which assumes, for example, that each observed variable represents a separate factor. They point out that "Since (the null model) can always be fit to any set of data without error, it does not represent a structural model that can be evaluated or rejected. Rather, it serves as a standard of comparison for," (595) other restricted models. This test, however, is so general that it may not be a particularly stringent one as pointed out by Hocevar Khattab, and Michael (1987). They recommend use of a one-factor model rather than the null model.

55 The difference in the degrees of freedom for the ML model is a result of having "fixed" a variance parameter to a value of one.

56 "A standardized residual is a fitted residual (as described earlier in this chapter) divided by the large-sample standard error of the residual," according to (Joreskog and Sorbom 1989, 28), who also recommended (1986) that such residuals be smaller than 2 for good models.

57 $t = 1.96$ is significant for large samples (N > 120)

58 These scores are coefficients from a regression of the latent variables on all of the observed variables as described by Joreskog and Sorbom (1989 131).

59 The coefficients are estimated by maximizing the likelihood (L) for the expression:

$$L(Y|X,B) = \prod_{i=1}^{n} \left[ \frac{\exp(\sum B_k X_{ik})}{1 + \exp(\sum B_k X_{ik})} \right]^{Y_i} \left[ \frac{1}{1 + \exp(\sum B_k X_{ik})} \right]^{1-Y_i}$$

Since the expressions are nonlinear in the parameters to be estimated, the Newton-Raphson algorithm is used to solve iteratively for the coefficients, B.

[60] This result is not unusual in studies using traditional dichotomous logit analysis (Stone and Rasp 1991) but has not been investigated with regard to multinomial logit. Stone and Rasp also find that in traditional logit analysis with samples of 100 or less "t-tests of individual variables are conservatively biased, and the test of the overall logit model is anticonservatively biased" (179). They find this problem to be most prevalent when data are skewed, as is often the case with accounting variables.

[61] The Chow test is a test for differences between the coefficients in OLS regression (Chow 1960), rather than multinomial logit models. OLS estimates were computed using the data from the current model for purposes of this test. The assumptions of OLS regression are violated when the dependent variable is categorical, as is the case here, due to heteroscedasticity. Toyoda (1974) points out, however, that the Chow test produces acceptable results under heteroscedasticity when sample sizes are large.

[62] These implications are discussed in the course of the analysis and in Chapter 5.

[63] Mann-Whitney U tests for differences in disclosure quality between categories of OC were not significant at conventional levels.

[64] In multinomial tests in which $mgr$ is entered as a cubic function, coefficients of the related independent variables were not significant at conventional levels.

[65] The low points in the curves representing MGR range from 28.5-30% for N=102, 32-45% for N=63 and 33.5-34% for N=165.

[66] The nonavailability of CRSP returns precludes computation of the STDEV variable. The remaining 9 firms were excluded from the original set because they did not report current assets and liabilities separately, so data items needed for the original LISREL model were not available.

[67] The y-axis represents the sum of P(DSCQ=2) and P(DSCQ=3) for the data set of 63 firms as noted earlier in the chapter)

[68] Note that the range of LNASSET for N=165 is greater than that for N=102, reflecting the observed ranges in the two data sets.

[69] Again, for N=63, P(DSCQ = 2 or 3) is used in these graphs.

# Chapter Five

# Conclusions, Limitations, Future Research Issues

This chapter presents a discussion of the conclusions to be drawn from the research findings presented in Chapter 4. Potential limitations of the methods and design employed in the study are discussed in the context of these findings. The chapter is organized into sections which pertain to the models specified and tests performed in the study. Each section includes a brief summary of the related findings. The discussion of conclusions and limitations is followed with suggestions for future research which could extend this line of inquiry. The chapter ends with a recapitulation of the conclusions in the context of their implications for public policy and for disclosure regulation.

## THE CREDIT RISK MODEL

Although factor analytical techniques have been used in past studies of financial distress and bankruptcy, this is the first known use of confirmatory factor analysis in a model of credit risk. The use of CFA was appropriate for this study in that the variables included in the models have each appeared in the literature, most repeatedly, as significant measures of the riskiness of the firm. CFA allows for the development and assessment of latent constructs representing the dimensions of credit risk which are not completely captured by any of the variables which are traditionally observed. Although the original specification of the model was based upon prior research findings in accounting, it was deficient as evidenced by its failure to converge in the estimation process. It is probable that the size of the sample was not sufficiently large for CFA when combined with the large number of variables to be estimated. In the respecified CFA model, fewer variables were used and other potential matters affecting "goodness of fit" were also addressed.

The set of variables selected for the respecified CFA model was consistent with evidence developed in past studies of credit risk. The new specification also incorporated both unique and market-related risk factors, which is a novel approach as implemented here, being based on the results of Marais, *et al* (1984). The new model exhibited a good fit in CFA and provided factor scores for the latent credit risk variables. Those scores were then used in tests of hypotheses related to disclosure quality. This allowed specification of the initial multinomial logit model using three latent credit risk variables, rather than the seven variables initially observed. The findings in the evaluation of the three-factor CFA model indicated that the seven variables in the data set provided acceptable measures of the size, unique risk, and market-related risk of the firms in the study.

## MULTINOMIAL LOGIT ANALYSIS

*The Full Model*

This study was initiated to consider the proposition that both the usage and the disclosure of interest rate swaps are related to the level of credit risk as well as the ownership structure of a firm. Examples of ways in which swap transactions can affect the risk profile of a firm, and associated incentives on the part of managers for limiting disclosure of these effects, were provided. It was argued that as a firm's ability to repay debts decreases (credit risk increases) managers have increased incentives to provide low quality swap disclosures. Since managers' incentives and intentions cannot be measured directly, the dependent variable tested is a measure of the quality of swap disclosures. This measure, DSCQ, serves as a proxy for managers' incentives and intentions to either disclose fully, or to withhold private information. Multinomial logit tests of DSCQ which included the three-factor measure of credit risk among the independent variables did not confirm the hypothesized relationship of DSCQ with credit risk.

A variety of potential explanations can be advanced, or conclusions drawn, based on the insignificance of tests for associations among variables. An obvious reason for the insignificance of credit risk variables in multinomial logit tests is that no relationship exists between a firm's credit risk profile and the quality of its disclosure.

Another is that the CFA model did not effectively measure the credit riskiness of firms in the sample. Arguments previously presented cast doubt upon these explanations, however. Several additional alternative explanations for the nonsignificance of the credit risk variables include the following:

(1) if managers act to avoid disclosure of increasing credit risk and they are successful, available information might not classify their firms in a higher risk category. In this case, these firms, identified as low risk firms in the credit risk model, would also exhibit low DSCQ - the opposite of the hypothesized relationship. For example, assume a firm's managers wish to increase long-term borrowing. If they then choose to use a combination of swaps and short term debt with the intention of continually rolling over the short-term debt, the new debt could be classified as long term under SFAS No. 6 (FASB 1975) and preserve the current ratio of the firm despite the additional short-term debt.

(2) managers of lower risk firms could have the same incentives as those in higher risk firms to withhold disclosure based on private information. Since their benefits from doing so would be comparatively smaller they are less likely to act opportunistically. To the extent that managers of low risk firms use low quality disclosure, however, ambiguity is introduced into the measures used here.

(3) high risk firms may be closed out of long term debt markets, and so their managers may be forced to use short term debt in order to obtain financing. In this case, the use of swaps in combination with the debt may be generally risk-reducing, and may entail no conflict of interests with shareholders. When no conflict is involved, managers would not have the motives for issuing low quality disclosure posited in this study. If managers generally use swaps and shorter term debt because other borrowing opportunities are not available, rather than by choice, then the effectiveness of the design of the current study would be reduced. That is, data arising from non-conflict situations might dominate the sample, making it impossible to measure the anticipated effects from conflict situations because they are underrepresented.

(4) the firms which disclosed swaps may have risk characteristics which are more homogeneous than those found in the general population, so that differences in levels of riskiness are difficult to detect statistically. The variance of the DRAT variable (.24 for N=102 and .25 for N=165) makes this explanation plausable.

(5) swaps are generally characterized in the literature (often by "financially sophisticated" authors) simply as risk-management instruments. Investors who are not aware of some of the negative implications of swap use which have been described in this study could be led to believe that swap use is indicative of a firm run by managers who are seeking a sophisticated form of risk reduction, thereby safeguarding owners' investments. This being the case, managers of high risk firms might have opportunistic incentives to provide high quality disclosure in order to become identified as users of sophisticated risk management techniques. The use of disclosure to mislead managers in this way would produce a situation contrary to that anticipated in this study.

(6) The measure of DSCQ may not reflect the risk characteristics of swap transactions to a sufficient degree to establish an association with the risk characteristics of the firm. That is, the measure used here is primarily an indicator of the level of compliance with generally accepted disclosure practices. Although a measure of DSCQ based primarily on current requirements and proposals is sufficient to serve as an indicator of underlying opportunistic behavior, even the highest quality disclosure based on these requirements may not fully capture swap-related risks.

*Ownership Structure Model*

The multinomial logit model (Figure 10), after having been respecified as an ownership structure model (Figure 11), was subject to an additional adjustment. The variable NOSH, representing the number of shareholders in the firm as a measure of diffusion of ownership, was also removed based on its insignificant, near-zero coefficient. There are plausible reasons for the lack of significance of NOSH in addition to the obvious possibility of no association. They include the following:

(1) NOSH is an ambiguous measure of the diffusion of ownership to the extent that even a very large number of individual shareholders could be aided in monitoring managers by either an individual or groups of shareholders controlling large stakes. The argument that as the number of shareholders grows, the cost of monitoring produces proportionally smaller rewards and thus is less likely to occur, might not hold if monitoring efforts were coordinated among shareholders. Significant holdings by activist shareholder

groups, large pension plans, or other institutional investors, for instance, could result in monitoring by representatives of these shareholder "pools". In this case, both the cost-effectiveness of monitoring activity and its frequency are likely to be improved as NOSH increases.

(2) There is a great deal of similarity between measures of diffusion and measures of size. That is, larger firms tend to have more shareholders, so LNASSET could serve as a proxy for NOSH in the model. This is borne out by the goodness of fit of the CFA model in which NOSH served as one of the observed measures of firm size. The two variables are significantly correlated.[70]

(3) As NOSH grows, the likelihood of having large individual ownership stakes diminishes, and smaller stakes generally will be sufficient to exercise control over managers. This makes NOSH a less effective indicator of control status as the number of shareholders increases.

*Owner Control and Leverage*

The revised ownership structure model employed in this study (Figure 12) includes variables which have traditionally been used to represent ownership structure as well as those which have served as control variables for size and leverage in the accounting/ownership structure literature. This model also provides the most highly significant set of findings in this study. Two of the independent variables in the model, OC (owner control) and DE (the debt/equity ratio), were not significant in any version of the model (102, 63 or 165) at any level of DSCQ.

In the case of DE, the nonsignificant coefficient estimate is consistent with the earlier results of the model which included credit risk variables. DE is an indicator of leverage, but highly leveraged firms are also generally higher credit risks, as they near or surpass a value-maximizing level of debt. The alternative explanations which were described above with regard to the non-significance of the credit risk variables, apply to the use of DE in the current model. Additional examples were presented in prior chapters. For instance, if swaps allow firms to increase current cash inflows without increasing debt on the balance sheet, in ways such as allowing for initial lump sum payments of the swap inflows, then DSCQ might reflect the transaction, but DE would not.

Although the coefficients for OC were not significant in the ownership structure models in this study, there are observable differences between graphs of the functions implied by multinomial logit analysis when OC = 0 and OC = 1. The differences between the disclosure quality depicted on these graphs reverse direction when comparing the original and full samples to the subset of 63 firms. That is, over the range of either LNASSET or MGR, for N=102 and N=165, DSCQ is consistently lower when OC = 1 (i.e. the firm is owner-controlled). If an owner with a stake of 5% or greater exercised effective control over managers, the opposite relationship would be expected. The opposite relationship does occur, however, when N=63. A 5% ownership stake (OC = 1) is related to higher DSCQ for these 63 firms. The differences in DSCQ between values of OC are also counterintuitive when size differences are considered. That is, the smaller average size of firms when N=63 would indicate that owners need a larger stake in order to exert control (and insist upon high quality disclosure), as compared with the owners in larger firms (N=102 or N=165). It is apparent that DSCQ reflects a difference in the extent of control exercised by 5% owners in the two sets of firms. One assertion which is reasonable based on this result is that the size of the ownership stake is not sufficient to determine the ability or likelihood of owners to control, but that other characteristics of ownership may be necessary as well. For example, a 5% owner who is part of a group which just participated in a takeover is more likely to exercise active control over management than the managers of a large mutual fund who manage a 5% stake, but who, as fiduciaries to investors, simply wish to maintain a balanced portfolio. The measure of OC used here and in the past does not distinguish between the two. Given the nature of the subsamples in this study, it is likely that such an effect is present here. That is, firms for which published returns or betas were not available are more likely to be younger firms, or to have been recently reorganized. The conflicting relationships between subsamples in the current study is also likely to have reduced the significance of OC in tests when N=165.

These findings point out potential shortcomings for the use of OC as a measure of owner control. OC overlaps with MGR to the extent that both reflect any ownership stake of 5% or greater which is held by a manager or director of the firm. This gives rise to covariation in the two measures when both are included in a study. In the study of Dhaliwal *et al*, OC serves as an indicator that a large owner controls the firm. This characterization of OC implies that if a manager were to hold a 5% ownership stake[71] the alignment effect might be expected to dominate beginning from the 5% ownership level. That is inconsistent with the implications of both current and past studies which demonstrate that the alignment effect is not dominant at MGR levels below 25-30%, or even higher levels for smaller firms. If OC is to serve as a measure of owner control, it must reflect the level of ownership at which corporate activity is consistent with owners' incentives. That is, the level at which owners have the ability to insure activity favorable to their interests by monitoring and discipline of managers. If the OC stake is owned by an outsider, it must be sufficient to allow exercise of effective control in favor of owners. If the OC stake is owned by a manager (or managers), it should reflect that percentage of ownership at which the convergence of interests occurs.

This is not a problem which is likely to be solved in a simple, universal manner due to the many ways in which control can be exercised. As pointed out by Morck, *et al* (1988), ownership by parties such as members of the board, founding families, managers, and even unusually persuasive individuals is likely to impact on activities within the firm in a variety of ways. Founding managers may be able to employ considerable control without retaining a sizable ownership stake, while large, passive, fiduciary investors (e.g. investment funds) may not attempt direct control of managerial activity. Further exploration of the OC variable and its relationship with other measures of corporate control are warranted.

## *Managerial Ownership and Firm Size*

The two remaining independent variables in the multinomial logit model, MGR and LNASSET, are the variables for which the estimated coefficients are significant in the models. As such, they are also the most instructive in terms of the conclusions which can be drawn based on test findings. As demonstrated in the graphs in Appendix D, the anticipated relationship between high quality disclosure and the percentage of management ownership is confirmed by the model. Moreover, the relationship is confirmed graphically in the functions implied by tests in the original group of 102, in the 63 additional firms, and in the pooled sample despite the lower significance level of the overall $X^2$ tests in the smaller and pooled groups. Statistically significant differences in the means of the independent variables between the two subsamples make it clear that the firms in the group of 63 are generally smaller, with greater levels of management ownership, and a higher incidence of cases in which there is at least one 5% owner. These 63 firms also have significantly higher DSCQ than the original group. The only coefficient estimate which is significant (at p=0.05) for N=63 is that of LNASSET, which indicates that the difference in size is the dominant difference between the two models.

Comparison of the graphs in Appendix D (and the underlying figures reported in Chapter 4) of the two functions shows that the lowest quality disclosure occurs at a higher level of managerial ownership (MGR) when N=63 than when N=102. This is consistent with the assumption that a larger ownership stake is needed to achieve control in a smaller firm. In this case, *the functions can be interpreted as an indication that* DSCQ *declines (the entrenchment effect dominates) to the point at which managers achieve effective control of the firm, after which increased managerial ownership coincides with increasing dominance of the alignment effect.*

Models representing both groups (102 and 63), as well as the pooled sample of 165 are consistent in that coefficients for MGR and $MGR^2$ have opposite signs, which indicate the nonlinearity of their relationship with DSCQ. These signs reverse, reflecting the opposite effects of P(DSCQ=1) and P(DSCQ=3) with regard to MGR. The drop in significance of $C^2$ for the pooled sample results in part from the greater similarity of the coefficients for the medium disclosure level, P(DSCQ=2), to P(DSCQ=3) for N=63, and to P(DSCQ=1) level for N=102. At the mid-level of DSCQ the coefficients have opposite signs for MGR and $MGR^2$ in the two subsamples, and the associated effects tend to cancel each other out in the pooled sample. Graphing the overall higher level of DSCQ for N=63 results in the familiar U-shaped curve only when the two higher probability levels are combined. This reflects the smaller size and higher DSCQ of the 63 firms. Test findings confirm that while these two groups of firms are very similar, they also differ in ways which can be anticipated based on the arguments in this study.

The importance of the relationship of firm size (as measured by LNASSET) with DSCQ is the other of the two most highly significant findings of this study. Again, the relationship is consistent across the two sub-samples and the pooled sample, with DSCQ declining as LNASSET increases. The decrease in DSCQ and underlying increase in opportunistic behavior it implies, is increasingly pervasive as firms increase in size.

The decrease in DSCQ is also consistent with the increased cost and difficulty of monitoring managers' activities as firms become larger. The use of both LNASSET and NOSH in an ownership structure model in which the size variable also measures diffusion of ownership is likely to account for the insignificance of NOSH in the original ownership structure model. The relationship between LNASSET and NOSH was confirmed by their joint representation of the size factor in CFA. Their association can also be characterized as a reflection of their relationships with the diffusion of ownership. The decrease in DSCQ as LNASSET increases is consistent with an increase in opportunistic behavior when monitoring becomes more difficult and costly and thus less likely to be carried out effectively.

## FUTURE RESEARCH ISSUES

*Disclosure Quality*

The measurement of the dependent variable, DSCQ, represents an original approach to analysis of disclosure by public companies. Its use in measuring the quality of disclosure is dependent upon the forms of disclosure currently in use by companies. These disclosures, in turn, reflect the current state of disclosure regulation, measurement and recognition customs and rules, and the level of understanding by both issuers and users of financial information of the characteristics and underlying implications of a transaction. The disclosure of a swap transaction, for example, may be more informative when presented in conjunction with descriptions of associated debt. The composition of DSCQ, and its effectiveness as a measure of disclosure quality, is limited by the extent of disclosure found in practice.

A weighting scheme for the elements of DSCQ which emphasized the disclosure elements which are most critical for measuring swap-related changes in firm risks might result in a more effective DSCQ measure. A potentially more promising approach would include the identification of additional disclosure elements which could shed greater light on the risk characteristics of swaps and thus improve the measurement of DSCQ. If those elements are currently not found in swap-related disclosures or requirements, they might be found elsewhere in a firm's disclosures, or be included in technical requirements of future disclosure regulation.

*Ownership Structure*

This study also raises questions about the effectiveness of OC as a measure of owner control. Although it has been a traditional measure of owner control in accounting research, it was not statistically significant in this study. Its effects could be observed, however, in graphs of the models implied by multinomial logit analysis.

A detailed analysis of owner-specific as well as firm-specific characteristics (and interactions between the two) holds potential for explaining systematic differences in the relationship of ownership to control across firms. Further exploration of variations in the composition of MGR and the overlap between MGR and OC, for example, would allow future researchers to ëliminate atypical control situations (outliers) and concentrate on broad, pervasive relationships. The development of a method for consistent classification of owners and managers, and their relative abilities to exert control in ways which affect the welfare of owners or investors could lead to a more effective measure of owner control.

The relationships among measures of firm size, the number of shareholders in a firm, and the diffusion of ownership are also entangled within accounting research studies. Measurement of diffusion is further complicated by institutional intermediaries. Exploration of the effects of these variables on corporate control also holds promise. Further exploration of the complexities of the separation of ownership and control has the potential to identify public policy implications and areas in which disclosure regulation might reduce disadvantages associated with managers' opportunistic behavior.

*Credit Risk and Confirmatory Factor Analysis*

The accounting literature provides many examples of studies which have been devised to study credit risk, financial distress, and the risk of bankruptcy. The original specification of the credit risk model in this study (Figure 2) reflected the diversity of measures used in the past, as well as the consistently significant results associated with a large number of them. The number of variables employed in the initial specification of the credit risk model in this study, however, resulted in too large a model for the relatively small number of swap disclosers identified. As a result, this study uses CFA in more of an "exploratory" or provisional sense than if the three factor model had been proposed originally. The resulting model, however, has the potential to serve as a general measure of credit risk in future research. The validity of the model as a measure of credit risk will be increased if similar studies performed using different data render similar results. In particular, a study in which the three credit risk factors identified here are tested as independent variables against an established indicator of credit risk or financial distress as the dependent variable, would confirm the external validity, or general nature, of the model.

## IMPLICATIONS FOR PUBLIC POLICY AND DISCLOSURE REGULATION

Research findings with regard to ownership structure imply that predicting the effects of owner control on managers requires more than knowledge of the size of the owners' stakes. For example, the aggregate level of managerial ownership appears to be more closely associated with changes in indicators of owners' welfare than the presense of large individual owners. Also, the set of assumptions and variables generally included in studies of ownership structure must be examined and adjusted to account for the number of legal owners who delegate control of their stakes. Their shares are then controlled by intermediaries with varying propensities to exercise corporate control. Thus the likelihood as well as the ability of owners to exercise control can be expected to depend on a number of factors not commonly addressed in accounting research. Characteristics of owners or their representatives, whether they are insiders or outsiders, individuals or institutions, those having the potential to initiate a takeover or cause shareholder unrest, or those who will "punt" and sell their shares at the first sign of trouble, are likely to be crucial in predicting the corporate control effects of their ownership. Although the names of owners holding stakes which equal or exceed 5% are now disclosed in the proxy statements of public firms, and the total percentage of shares owned by managers and directors is also disclosed, this information may fall short of that needed by investors to predict the effects of corporate ownership and control on their welfare.

The results of tests of the relationships between DSCQ and both MGR and LNASSET are consistent with predictions based on a conflict of interests between managers and investors. Test findings also confirm the results of past studies which identified a nonlinear relationship between management ownership levels and a variety of indicators of shareholder and investor welfare. The results here indicate that the quality of swap disclosure declines with increases in the size of the firm. DSCQ also declines with increases in managerial ownership over the range beneath which managers are generally assumed to lack overall control of the firm, and it increases thereafter. The implication underlying these patterns of disclosure quality is that there is a reason for declining quality of disclosure - opportunistic behavior on the part of managers.

Limitations in the measure of DSCQ which are directly related to the extent of current swap disclosure add to the concern that these current disclosures are inadequate. That is, that they do not fully disclose the potential for associated changes in the risk profile of firms, even when the quality of disclosure is high. A better measure of DSCQ might be developed with further investigation of the available ways to use swaps as well as the ways in which swaps are used, the relative frequencies with which different uses occur, and the risks involved in each. The systematic variation in the quality of current disclosures with MGR, however, indicates that concern about adequate disclosure and, relatedly, the welfare of those who rely on public disclosure of swap transactions is well-founded.

# Notes

[70] The correlation between NOSH and LNASSET (.635) is significant at the level p=0.000.

[71] Dhaliwal, *et al* ignored ownership stakes between the sizes of 5 and 10%. Based on their criteria, then, they might be expected to assume the alignment effect would dominate at ownership levels exceeding 10%.

# Appendix A

## DESCRIPTION OF AN INTEREST RATE SWAP
## TRANSACTION

The following description of a standard (generally known as a "plain vanilla") swap transaction is adapted from an example presented by John E. Stewart, a partner in the firm of Arthur Andersen & Co., at an Accounting and Auditing Symposium held on October 18, 1988. This type of example has become a traditional feature of writings which deal with interest rate swaps. It is also commonly used to demonstrate the traditional economic justification of swaps based on the notion of comparative advantage of the firms in fixed vs floating rate markets.

An interest rate swap involves two parties. One of the parties is commonly an intermediary party which then may match the swap with another swap transaction, but all basic swaps involve two parties. Of the two parties, one will have a higher credit rating (a lower risk firm - often a bank) than the other (a firm with a higher level of credit risk and thus a lower rating.)

Typically, the lower rated firm prefers borrowing at a fixed interest rate (to avoid the risk of market fluctuations in interest rates on floating rate debt.) This firm may be unable to access the fixed rate market or unwilling to pay the high interest rates it would incur in doing so, and so will borrow either in the floating rate (as in this example) or the short term markets.

The higher rated firm which is a party to this swap will have incentives to borrow in the floating rate market. This firm will have access to both the fixed and floating rate markets at more favorable rates than the lower rated firm due to its risk characteristics. If the firm borrows in the fixed rate market, it can then engage in an interest rate swap with the lower rated firm and, in addition to ending up with the preferred floating rate debt, collect a premium over and above the amount needed to cover the cost of its original financing.

An interest rate swap such as the one just described is illustrated below. In this case the low rated firm has the options of borrowing fixed at 17%, or floating at LIBOR (see note 19) plus an additional 3/4%. Its managers choose to borrow from the floating rate lender. The higher rated firm can borrow fixed at 12 1/2% and from the floating rate lender at LIBOR. Its management chooses to borrow fixed and swap with the lower rated firm, charging a premium of 3 1/2% on notional principal.

As illustrated, the firms agree to pay based on the obligations of the other party to the swap. The low rated firm pays 16% of notional principal (12 1/2% which covers the other party's obligation and a 3 1/2% premium) to the high rated firm. The notional principal does not change hands, and typically just the net of the payments owed by the parties will change hands on payment dates. The effect for the low rated firm, is that its payments on its underlying floating rate debt are met by the swap receipts, and the amount it pays for its borrowings is based on an effective rate of 16%. This is one percentage point less than it could have borrowed for without the swap.    The higher rated firm, in turn, receives the interest needed to service its fixed rate debt as well as a premium based on the notional principal.

## EXAMPLE OF AN INTEREST RATE SWAP
## TRANSACTION

(arrows indicate cash flows)

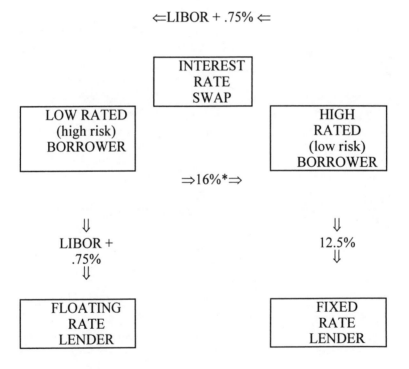

⇐LIBOR + .75% ⇐

| INTEREST RATE SWAP |
|---|

| LOW RATED (high risk) BORROWER | | HIGH RATED (low risk) BORROWER |
|---|---|---|

⇒16%*⇒

⇓ LIBOR + .75% ⇓          ⇓ 12.5% ⇓

| FLOATING RATE LENDER | | FIXED RATE LENDER |
|---|---|---|

*16%=12.5%+3.5%PREMIUM TO HIGH RATED FIRM

# Appendix B

## REQUIREMENTS FOR DISCLOSURE OF INFORMATION ABOUT FINANCIAL INSTRUMENTS WITH OFF-BALANCE-SHEET RISK[1] AND FINANCIAL INSTRUMENTS WITH CONCENTRATIONS OF CREDIT RISK

## STATEMENT OF FINANCIAL ACCOUNTING STANDARDS NO. 105 (FASB 1990)

"For financial instruments with off-balance-sheet risk,...an entity shall disclose either in the body of the financial statements or in the accompanying notes the following information by class of financial instrument:[2]

a.      The face or contract amount (or notional principal amount if there is no face or contract amount)

b.      The nature and terms, including, at a minimum, a discussion of (1) the credit and market risk of those instruments, (2) the cash requirements of those instruments, and (3) the related accounting policy pursuant to the requirements of APB Opinion No. 22, *Disclosure of Accounting Policies*," (p. 7, par. 17).

"For financial instruments with off-balance-sheet credit risk...an entity shall disclose either in the body of the financial statements or in the accompanying notes the following information by class of financial instrument:

a.      The amount of accounting loss the entity would incur if any party to the financial instrument failed completely to perform according to the terms of the contract and the collateral or other security, if any, for the amount due proved to be of no value to the entity

b.      The entity's policy of requiring collateral or other security to support financial instruments subject to credit risk, information about the entity's access to that collateral or other security, and the nature and a brief description of the collateral or other security supporting those financial instruments," (p. 8, par. 18).

"An entity may find that disclosing additional information about the extent of collateral or other security for the underlying instrument indicates better the extent of credit risk. Disclosure of that additional information in those circumstances is encouraged," (p. 8, par. 19).

"an entity shall disclose all significant concentrations of credit risk arising from *all* financial instruments, whether from an individual counterparty or groups of counterparties. *Group concentrations* of credit risk exist if a number of counterparties are engaged in similar activities and have similar economic characteristics that would cause their ability to meet contractual obligations to be similarly affected by changes in economic or other conditions. The following shall be disclosed about each significant concentration:

a.      Information about the (shared activity, region, or economic characteristic that identifies the concentration

b.     The amount of the accounting loss due to credit risk the entity would incur if parties to the financial instruments that make up the concentration failed completely to perform according to the terms of the contracts and the collateral or other security, if any, for the amount due proved to be of no value to the entity

c.     The entity's policy of requiring collateral or other security to support financial instruments subject to credit risk, information about the entity's access to that collateral or other security, and the nature and a brief description of the collateral or other security supporting those financial instruments," (pp. 8-9, par. 20).

# Notes

[1] Interest rate swap contracts are singled out as financial instruments having off-balance-sheet risk in an example in paragraph 8, page 4, and also in paragraph 13 of SFAS 105.

[2] "Practices for grouping and separately identifying--classifying--similar financial instruments in statements of financial position, in notes to financial statements, and in various regulatory reports have developed and become generally accepted, largely without being codified in authoritative literature. In this Statement, *class of financial instrument* refers to those classifications," (p. 7, n. 12).

# Appendix C

## 102 FIRMS IN ORIGINAL DATA SET

| NAME | DSCQ | MGR | TOT ASSET | OC | DE | NOSH |
|---|---|---|---|---|---|---|
| AMR CORP | 3 | 0.002 | 9722.398 | 0 | 1.9480 | 20800 |
| AMAX INC. | 1 | 0.470 | 4076.000 | 1 | 1.3868 | 20549 |
| AMERICAN BUSINESS PRODUCTS | 1 | 30.200 | 152.257 | 1 | 0.6003 | 1900 |
| AMES DEPARTMENT STORES | 1 | 1.800 | 2129.564 | 0 | 2.5421 | 6082 |
| ARMSTRONG WORLD IND. | 3 | 1.040 | 2097.699 | 0 | 1.0529 | 10355 |
| ASARCO INC | 3 | 1.130 | 2223.363 | 1 | 0.6708 | 15000 |
| AVERY INTERNATIONAL CORP | 3 | 16.600 | 1119.100 | 1 | 1.1969 | 4149 |
| AVON PRODUCTS INC | 2 | 3.300 | 2460.400 | 0 | 9.2817 | 35100 |
| BADGER METER INC | 3 | 78.100 | 41.787 | 1 | 0.7429 | 788 |
| BARNES GROUP INC | 2 | 27.000 | 311.876 | 1 | 1.3307 | 3259 |
| BLACK & DECKER CORP. | 3 | 1.200 | 1825.109 | 0 | 1.5178 | 19820 |
| BURLINGTON NORTHERN INC | 3 | 0.280 | 6330.332 | 0 | 5.7913 | 36669 |
| CNW CORPORATION | 3 | 6.970 | 1726.991 | 0 | 1.7130 | 5005 |
| CASTLE & CO (A M) | 3 | 22.110 | 211.885 | 1 | 2.2333 | 1732 |

| NAME | DSCQ | MGR | TOT ASSET | OC | DE | NOSH |
|------|------|-----|-----------|----|----|------|
| CENTRAL MAINE POWER CO | | | | | | |
| | 3 | 0.189 | 1211.129 | 0 | 1.9473 | 40128 |
| CHEMED CORP | | | | | | |
| | 1 | 5.010 | 322.679 | 1 | 1.9006 | 2653 |
| CIRCLE K CORP | | | | | | |
| | 1 | 22.300 | 2044.940 | 1 | 4.4114 | 4700 |
| CIRCUS CIRCUS | | | | | | |
| | 3 | 51.800 | 524.112 | 1 | 2.6168 | 2341 |
| COASTAL CORP | | | | | | |
| | 3 | 5.960 | 7865.296 | 0 | 5.1839 | 38000 |
| COLUMBIA GAS SYSTEM INC | | | | | | |
| | 3 | 0.260 | 5641.000 | 0 | 2.6333 | 92770 |
| CONNECTICUT NAT GAS CORP | | | | | | |
| | 1 | 1.800 | 327.003 | 0 | 2.4861 | 9616 |
| CONQUEST EXPLORATION CO | | | | | | |
| | 3 | 6.700 | 140.023 | 1 | 0.8771 | 8500 |
| CROMPTON & KNOWLES CORP | | | | | | |
| | 2 | 5.600 | 205.642 | 1 | 1.5102 | 2200 |
| DALLAS CORP | | | | | | |
| | 1 | 9.800 | 202.547 | 1 | 1.1005 | 1440 |
| DUN & BRADSTREET | | | | | | |
| | 3 | 3.080 | 5023.755 | 0 | 1.4000 | 17433 |
| EASTMAN KODAK CO | | | | | | |
| | 1 | 0.000 | 22964.003 | 0 | 2.3870 | 174110 |
| EDISON BROTHERS STORES INC | | | | | | |
| | 2 | 27.341 | 512.700 | 1 | 1.4082 | 4800 |
| EMERSON ELECTRIC CO. | | | | | | |
| | 1 | 1.600 | 5027.000 | 0 | 0.7826 | 35800 |
| EMHART | | | | | | |
| | 1 | 0.000 | 2426.600 | 0 | 1.4993 | 18846 |
| ENGELHARD CORP | | | | | | |
| | 1 | 2.510 | 1413.155 | 1 | 0.8585 | 11791 |
| ENRON INC | | | | | | |
| | 1 | 4.650 | 8694.804 | 1 | 3.9994 | 29995 |
| ENSERCH CORP | | | | | | |
| | 3 | 1.140 | 2970.118 | 0 | 3.0220 | 28534 |

| NAME | DSCQ | MGR | TOT ASSET | OC | DE | NOSH |
|------|------|-----|-----------|----|----|------|
| FMC | 2 | 3.900 | 2748.751 | 1 | -13.2906 | 19155 |
| FABRI CENTERS OF AMERICA INC | 1 | 32.500 | 134.553 | 1 | 1.2594 | 900 |
| FEDERAL PAPER BOARD CO INC | 1 | 7.100 | 1335.334 | 0 | 1.0822 | 5872 |
| FOSTER WHEELER CORP | 3 | 1.898 | 1108.557 | 1 | 1.4574 | 10660 |
| FOXBORO CO | 1 | 16.347 | 472.235 | 1 | 1.4194 | 3786 |
| FREEPORT MCMORAN INC | 1 | 4.300 | 3729.7710 | 1 | 2.4234 | 22754 |
| GENCORP INC | 3 | 0.500 | 1230.000 | 1 | -35.1667 | 16800 |
| GENERAL HOST CORP | 1 | 11.100 | 532.656 | 1 | 2.1037 | 4742 |
| GENERAL SIGNAL CORP | 3 | 0.900 | 1396.600 | 0 | 2.0292 | 15500 |
| GEORGIA PACIFIC CORP | 3 | 1.900 | 7115.000 | 0 | 1.7002 | 53000 |
| GLATFELTER CO (P H) | 2 | 24.300 | 663.048 | 1 | 0.9748 | 3219 |
| GOODYEAR TIRE & RUBBER CO | 1 | 0.900 | 8618.296 | 0 | 3.2515 | 46162 |
| GREAT NORTHERN NEKOOSA CORP | 1 | 0.700 | 3821.400 | 0 | 1.4929 | 19605 |
| HASBRO INC | 2 | 28.000 | 1111.908 | 1 | 0.5812 | 5500 |
| HASTINGS MANUFACTURING CO | 1 | 18.280 | 45.318 | 1 | 1.2578 | 520 |
| HORN & HARDART CO | 2 | 39.176 | 363.328 | 1 | 4.1372 | 2295 |
| IOWA ILLINOIS GAS & ELECTRIC | 2 | 2.580 | 1242.421 | 0 | 1.7530 | 24190 |
| KANSAS CITY POWER & LIGHT CO | 1 | 0.990 | 2647.414 | 0 | 1.9242 | 32601 |

| NAME | DSCQ | MGR | TOT ASSET | OC | DE | NOSH |
|---|---|---|---|---|---|---|
| KROGER CO. (THE) | | | | | | |
| | 2 | 3.000 | 4613.996 | 0 | -2.7227 | 60964 |
| LAFARGE CORP | | | | | | |
| | 3 | 1.010 | 1199.408 | 1 | 0.7559 | 11300 |
| LOCKHEED CORP | | | | | | |
| | 2 | 1.500 | 6643.000 | 0 | 1.6830 | 14154 |
| M/A-COM INC | | | | | | |
| | 1 | 1.810 | 482.812 | 0 | 1.2203 | 14200 |
| MAPCO INC | | | | | | |
| | 3 | 4.796 | 1375.553 | 0 | 1.2529 | 5900 |
| MARRIOTT CORP | | | | | | |
| | 2 | 14.080 | 5981.000 | 1 | 7.4239 | 55606 |
| MAY DEPARTMENT STORES CO | | | | | | |
| | 1 | 0.463 | 6181.000 | 0 | 1.2674 | 48744 |
| MCDONALD'S CORP | | | | | | |
| | 1 | 1.462 | 8158.671 | 1 | 1.3906 | 63300 |
| MEAD CORP | | | | | | |
| | 1 | 3.400 | 3540.499 | 0 | 1.2587 | 23300 |
| MEDIA GENERAL INC | | | | | | |
| | 2 | 14.520 | 859.014 | 1 | 2.4031 | 3083 |
| NALCO CHEMICAL CO | | | | | | |
| | 3 | 1.800 | 838.857 | 0 | 0.7567 | 5477 |
| NATIONAL MEDICAL ENTERPRISES | | | | | | |
| | 2 | 5.200 | 3507.000 | 0 | 2.6455 | 15000 |
| NEW JERSEY RESOURCES CORP | | | | | | |
| | 3 | 0.797 | 458.353 | 0 | 2.0722 | 15110 |
| NIAGARA MOHAWK POWER CORP | | | | | | |
| | 3 | 0.191 | 7076.041 | 0 | 1.8684 | 162000 |
| ONEIDA LTD | | | | | | |
| | 3 | 3.200 | 236.961 | 1 | 1.5887 | 6114 |
| OWENS & MINOR INC | | | | | | |
| | 3 | 11.200 | 189.916 | 1 | 1.4610 | 3900 |
| PHH GROUP, INC. | | | | | | |
| | 1 | 1.490 | 4148.137 | 0 | 12.1280 | 3028 |
| PEPSICO INC | | | | | | |
| | 2 | 0.386 | 11135.300 | 0 | 2.5227 | 94000 |

| NAME | DSCQ | MGR | TOT ASSET | OC | DE | NOSH |
|------|------|-----|-----------|----|----|------|
| PHILLIPS PETROLEUM CO | | | | | | |
| | 1 | 0.533 | 11968.000 | 1 | 4.6640 | 96900 |
| PHILLIPS VAN HEUSEN CORP | | | | | | |
| | 3 | 18.700 | 323.133 | 1 | 2.0694 | 2383 |
| PORTLAND GENERAL CORP | | | | | | |
| | 1 | 0.096 | 2511.219 | 0 | 1.4277 | 61576 |
| QANTEL CORP. | | | | | | |
| | 3 | 22.200 | 47.790 | 1 | -2.0907 | 7711 |
| RALSTON PURINA CO | | | | | | |
| | 3 | 6.310 | 4044.400 | 0 | 2.7108 | 32475 |
| REYNOLDS METALS CO | | | | | | |
| | 2 | 5.138 | 5031.695 | 0 | 1.4664 | 13155 |
| ROGERS CORPORATION | | | | | | |
| | 3 | 8.126 | 108.069 | 0 | 1.0273 | 1453 |
| SCOTT PAPER CO | | | | | | |
| | 1 | 1.196 | 5156.296 | 0 | 1.6417 | 44200 |
| SOUTHDOWN INC | | | | | | |
| | 3 | 1.850 | 1210.778 | 0 | 2.2535 | 2532 |
| SOUTHWESTERN ENERGY CO | | | | | | |
| | 3 | 1.210 | 311.632 | 0 | 2.3112 | 3426 |
| SPRINGS INDUSTRIES INC | | | | | | |
| | 1 | 1.890 | 1118.257 | 1 | 1.0647 | 3700 |
| SUN ELECTRIC CORP | | | | | | |
| | 1 | 2.100 | 160.462 | 1 | 1.1290 | 2697 |
| SUPER FOOD SERVICES INC | | | | | | |
| | 3 | 11.048 | 224.439 | 0 | 1.3989 | 1881 |
| SYNTEX CORP | | | | | | |
| | 1 | 1.900 | 1443.700 | 0 | 0.9152 | 18200 |
| TRW INC | | | | | | |
| | 3 | 1.400 | 4442.000 | 1 | 1.8365 | 38200 |
| TALLEY INDUSTRIES INC | | | | | | |
| | 2 | 10.070 | 533.300 | 0 | 2.7574 | 3560 |
| TENNECO INC | | | | | | |
| | 1 | 0.197 | 17376.003 | 0 | 4.1181 | 160917 |
| THERMO ELECTRON CORP | | | | | | |
| | 3 | 0.000 | 490.109 | 0 | 1.7002 | 4759 |

| NAME | DSCQ | MGR | TOT ASSET | OC | DE | NOSH |
|---|---|---|---|---|---|---|
| THOMAS & BETTS CORP | | | | | | |
| | 3 | 6.900 | 492.942 | 0 | 0.5658 | 5243 |
| TIME INC. | | | | | | |
| | 3 | 0.000 | 4913.000 | 0 | 2.6152 | 14799 |
| TIMES MIRROR COMPANY (THE) | | | | | | |
| | 1 | 48.440 | 3475.609 | 1 | 1.0604 | 5461 |
| TOSCO | | | | | | |
| | 1 | 53.490 | 556.283 | 1 | 1.0695 | 34723 |
| TOTAL PETROLEUM NORTH AMERICA | | | | | | |
| | 2 | 0.490 | 962.903 | 1 | 1.5335 | 5000 |
| UGI CORP | | | | | | |
| | 2 | 1.240 | 619.383 | 0 | 1.4601 | 17809 |
| USG CORP | | | | | | |
| | 1 | 1.350 | 1821.178 | 0 | -2.2381 | 14713 |
| UNION CARBIDE CORP | | | | | | |
| | 3 | 0.400 | 8441.000 | 0 | 3.5975 | 66491 |
| U S AIR GROUP INC | | | | | | |
| | 2 | 0.969 | 5348.875 | 0 | 1.5846 | 24357 |
| VALERO ENERGY CORP | | | | | | |
| | 1 | 2.250 | 926.517 | 0 | 0.7568 | 15283 |
| VIACOM INC | | | | | | |
| | 1 | 83.000 | 3980.054 | 1 | 4.0598 | 8606 |
| WESTERN CO OF NORTH AMERICA | | | | | | |
| | 1 | 7.060 | 534.273 | 0 | -3.2944 | 14900 |
| WESTINGHOUSE ELECTRIC CORP | | | | | | |
| | 2 | 0.384 | 16937.304 | 0 | 3.4637 | 112774 |
| WHIRLPOOL CORP | | | | | | |
| | 2 | 2.900 | 3409.699 | 0 | 1.5813 | 12521 |
| WILLIAMS COMPANIES INC | | | | | | |
| | 1 | 3.800 | 3566.800 | 1 | 2.1626 | 9935 |
| ZAPATA CORP | | | | | | |
| | 1 | 5.066 | 771.412 | 0 | -67.1475 | 14193 |

## 63 FIRMS ADDED TO DATA SET

| NAME | DSCQ | MGR | TOT ASSET | OC | DE | NOSH |
|---|---|---|---|---|---|---|
| ADAMS RUSSELL ELECTRONICS CO | | | | | | |
| | 2 | 10.228 | 141.882 | 1 | 0.8187 | 1312 |
| ALBANY INTERNATIONAL CORP | | | | | | |
| | 3 | 74.710 | 477.237 | 1 | 1.6774 | 3800 |
| AMERICAN MAGNETICS | | | | | | |
| | 3 | 30.690 | 34.441 | 1 | 0.5467 | 945 |
| AMERICAN TELEVISION & COMMUNICATIONS | | | | | | |
| | 3 | 0.194 | 1508.424 | 1 | 4.6733 | 946 |
| CABLEVISION SYSTEMS CORP | | | | | | |
| | 3 | 53.900 | 1170.858 | 1 | -5.6635 | 372 |
| CARE ENTERPRISES | | | | | | |
| | 1 | 51.852 | 215.465 | 1 | -7.8350 | 1216 |
| CENTURY COMM. CORP | | | | | | |
| | 3 | 97.400 | 557.009 | 1 | 51.7822 | 415 |
| CHRYSLER CORP | | | | | | |
| | 1 | 1.026 | 48566.81 | 0 | 5.4053 | 205807 |
| CINEPLEX ODEON | | | | | | |
| | 3 | 21.810 | 1263.171 | 1 | 2.3690 | 1330 |
| COCA COLA BOTTLING CO. CONSOLIDATED | | | | | | |
| | 3 | 72.360 | 399.599 | 1 | 1.9234 | 1298 |
| CONTINENTAL MATERIALS | | | | | | |
| | 3 | 24.200 | 65.765 | 1 | 0.1046 | 4000 |
| EL PASO ELECTRIC CO | | | | | | |
| | 2 | 0.340 | 1975.158 | 0 | 2.0490 | 43535 |
| FULLER (H B) | | | | | | |
| | 2 | 27.900 | 434.293 | 1 | 1.4280 | 2970 |
| GENERAL HOMES CORP | | | | | | |
| | 3 | 74.700 | 437.593 | 1 | 66.1670 | 621 |
| GRACE & CO (W R) | | | | | | |
| | 1 | 6.700 | 5310.296 | 0 | 2.4236 | 27012 |
| GREYHOUND CORP | | | | | | |
| | 3 | 1.200 | 5033.875 | 1 | 3.9905 | 67175 |
| HARCOURT BRACE JOVAN. INC | | | | | | |
| | 3 | 6.300 | 3232.541 | 1 | -4.6822 | 5679 |

| NAME | DSCQ | MGR | TOT ASSET | OC | DE | NOSH |
|------|------|------|-----------|-----|------|------|
| HEILIG MEYERS CO | | | | | | |
| | 2 | 5.700 | 499.198 | 0 | 2.2130 | 2200 |
| HIMONT INC | | | | | | |
| | 1 | 0.300 | 1904.955 | 1 | 0.4027 | 7900 |
| IMC FERTILIZER GROUP INC | | | | | | |
| | 1 | 0.900 | 1472.100 | 1 | 1.1773 | 126 |
| IMO INDUSTRIES | | | | | | |
| | 3 | 1.800 | 756.007 | 1 | 1.5634 | 44095 |
| INACOMP COMPUTER CENTERS | | | | | | |
| | 1 | 31.800 | 94.967 | 1 | 1.5701 | 1015 |
| INCO LTD | | | | | | |
| | 3 | 0.040 | 4078.848 | 0 | 4.3159 | 41000 |
| INFINITY BROADCASTING | | | | | | |
| | 3 | 92.680 | 235.252 | 1 | 10.2228 | 2000 |
| INTEL CORP | | | | | | |
| | 1 | 10.421 | 3549.736 | 1 | 0.7066 | 20154 |
| INVACARE | | | | | | |
| | 3 | 48.400 | 102.288 | 1 | 2.3939 | 1276 |
| KIRSHNER MEDICAL CORP | | | | | | |
| | 1 | 10.800 | 73.935 | 0 | 1.6588 | 1711 |
| LENNAR CORP | | | | | | |
| | 1 | 83.500 | 509.764 | 1 | 1.1980 | 1100 |
| LOWE'S COMPANIES INC | | | | | | |
| | 3 | 5.203 | 1085.797 | 1 | 0.8502 | 6602 |
| MAGMA COPPER | | | | | | |
| | 2 | 1.040 | 890.379 | 1 | 1.2856 | 7601 |
| McCORMICK & CO, INC. | | | | | | |
| | 3 | 1.750 | 770.178 | 1 | 1.6171 | 1456 |
| METRO MOBILE CTS | | | | | | |
| | 3 | 50.920 | 241.935 | 1 | -10.5421 | 482 |
| MOR-FLO INDUSTRIES, INC. | | | | | | |
| | 1 | 72.500 | 129.986 | 1 | 2.6657 | 586 |
| MULTIMEDIA INC. | | | | | | |
| | 2 | 16.580 | 405.000 | 1 | -1.7548 | 1200 |
| NOVA CORP OF ALBERTA | | | | | | |
| | 3 | 0.211 | 6910.089 | 0 | 3.0402 | 38400 |

| NAME | DSCQ | MGR | TOT ASSET | OC | DE | NOSH |
|------|------|-----|-----------|----|----|------|
| OGLEBAY NORTON CO | | | | | | |
| | 1 | 13.730 | 254.297 | 1 | 1.1035 | 870 |
| PACIFIC ENTERPRISES | | | | | | |
| | 2 | 1.500 | 6866.000 | 1 | 2.4261 | 62966 |
| PACIFIC TELECOM | | | | | | |
| | 2 | 0.156 | 1242.378 | 1 | 1.7211 | 4908 |
| PACIFICORP | | | | | | |
| | 1 | 0.168 | 11396.10 | 0 | 2.5189 | 188000 |
| PENTAIR | | | | | | |
| | 2 | 5.100 | 744.664 | 1 | 1.6430 | 3036 |
| PIONEER-STANDARD ELECTRONICS | | | | | | |
| | 2 | 9.600 | 126.946 | 1 | 2.7572 | 621 |
| SAVANNAH FOODS | | | | | | |
| | 2 | 7.100 | 395.133 | 1 | 1.9383 | 2525 |
| SCHERER (R P) | | | | | | |
| | 2 | 64.300 | 327.263 | 1 | 1.2169 | 1029 |
| SCHULMAN (A) | | | | | | |
| | 3 | 12.900 | 240.475 | 1 | 0.6564 | 1060 |
| SCRIPPS CO (E W) | | | | | | |
| | 2 | 98.500 | 1556.314 | 1 | 1.4777 | 2022 |
| SEARS ROEBUCK & CO | | | | | | |
| | 3 | 0.310 | 77951.56 | 1 | 4.5462 | 351999 |
| SHONEY'S INC | | | | | | |
| | 2 | 32.310 | 403.560 | 1 | -2.0642 | 8358 |
| SONOCO PRODUCTS | | | | | | |
| | 3 | 8.860 | 977.459 | 0 | 1.1507 | 21500 |
| SPAN-AMERICA MEDICAL SYSTEMS | | | | | | |
| | 2 | 32.467 | 13.416 | 0 | 0.8547 | 555 |
| SUBARU OF AMERICA | | | | | | |
| | 1 | 1.300 | 727.716 | 1 | 2.4693 | 5955 |
| SUNRISE MEDICAL | | | | | | |
| | 3 | 29.660 | 116.717 | 1 | 3.6659 | 355 |
| SYRACUSE SUPPLY | | | | | | |
| | 3 | 38.270 | 94.439 | 1 | 3.2686 | 742 |
| TCA CABLE TV | | | | | | |
| | 3 | 55.100 | 135.432 | 1 | 1.2781 | 1600 |

| NAME | DSCQ | MGR | TOT ASSET | OC | DE | NOSH |
|------|------|-----|-----------|----|----|------|
| TELE COMMUNICATIONS INC | | | | | | |
| | 1 | 45.229 | 8574.00 | 1 | 6.1124 | 4751 |
| TEXTRON INC | | | | | | |
| | 3 | 1.050 | 12554.1 | 1 | 4.2640 | 36000 |
| THORN APPLE VALLEY | | | | | | |
| | 2 | 71.900 | 102.994 | 1 | 2.0391 | 903 |
| TOWN & COUNTRY CORP | | | | | | |
| | 3 | 85.232 | 317.223 | 1 | 2.9156 | 474 |
| TRIBUNE CO | | | | | | |
| | 3 | 22.000 | 2941.58 | 1 | 1.4751 | 3200 |
| WATTS INDUSTRIES INC | | | | | | |
| | 3 | 89.800 | 176.760 | 1 | 0.4377 | 275 |
| WESTMARC COMMUN. INC. | | | | | | |
| | 1 | 21.366 | 601.480 | 1 | 4.1088 | 2649 |
| WETTERAU INC | | | | | | |
| | 3 | 23.400 | 952.123 | 1 | 3.1388 | 6088 |
| WEYERHAEUSER CO | | | | | | |
| | 3 | 0.000 | 15387.1 | 0 | 2.8042 | 30379 |
| XEROX CORP | | | | | | |
| | 3 | 0.704 | 26441.01 | 0 | 3.6658 | 84864 |

# Appendix D

# CHANGES IN P(DSCQ=3) OVER RANGE OF MGR

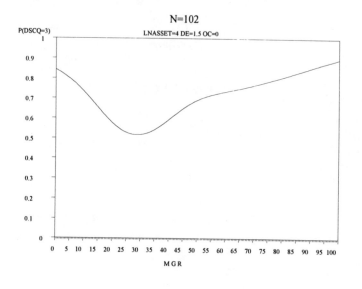

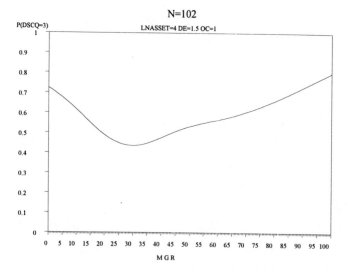

N=102

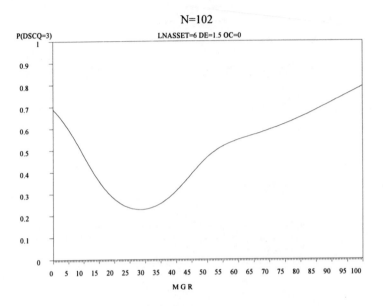

N=102

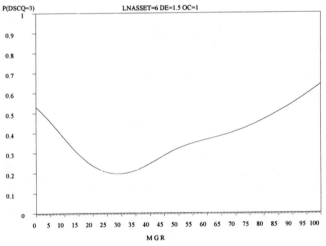

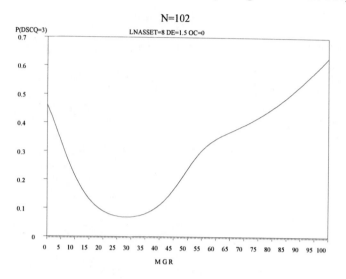

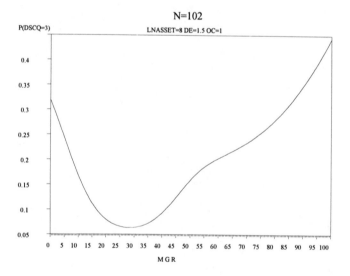

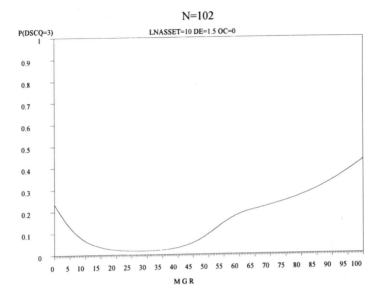

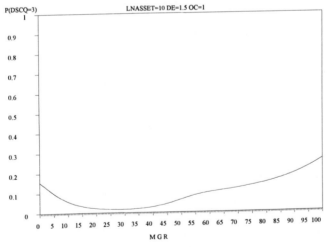

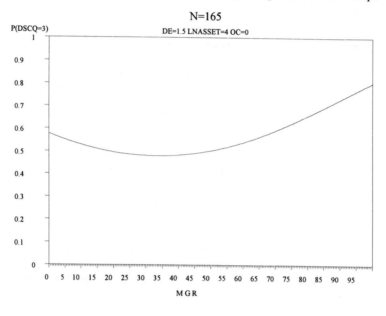

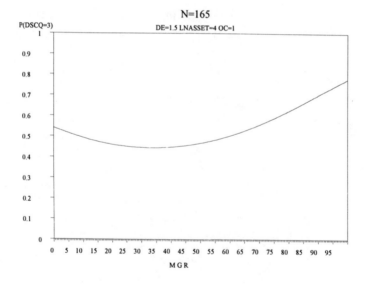

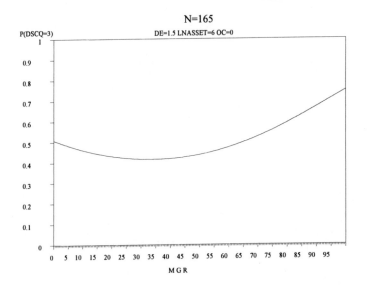

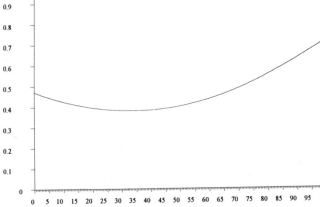

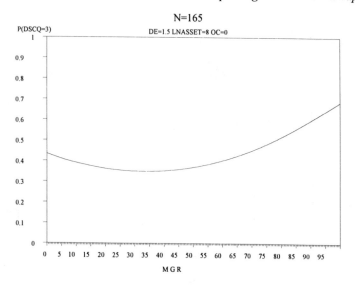

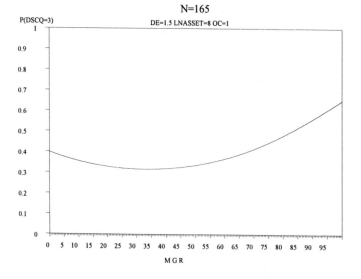

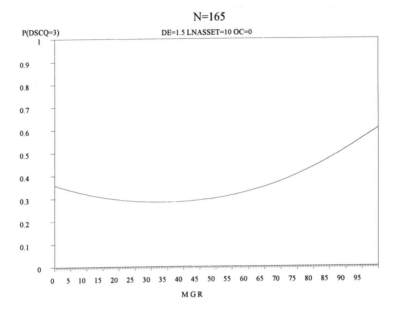

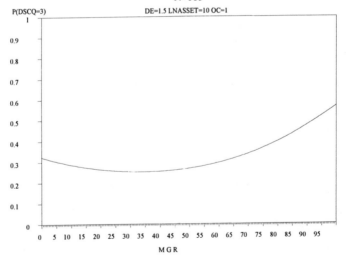

# CHANGES IN P(DSCQ=2 OR 3) OVER RANGE OF MGR

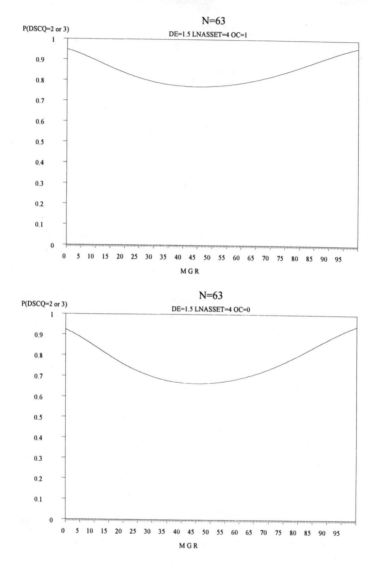

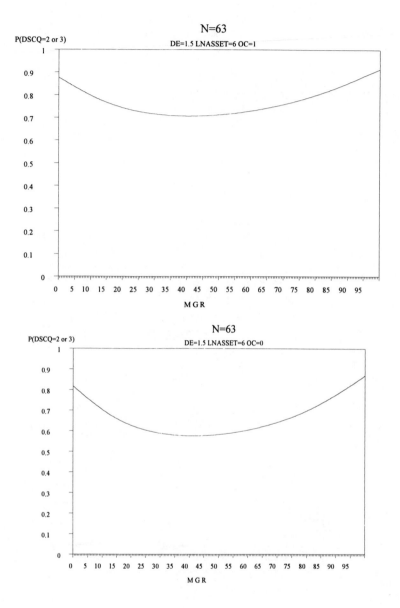

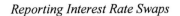

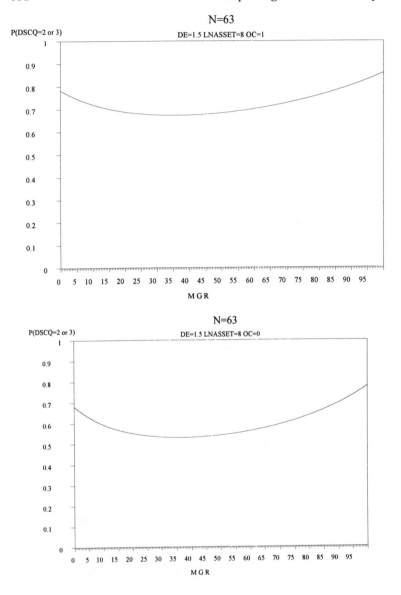

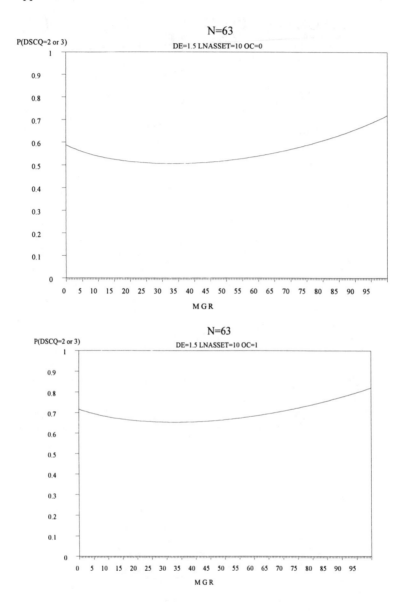

# CHANGES IN P(DSCQ=3) OVER RANGES OF LNASSET

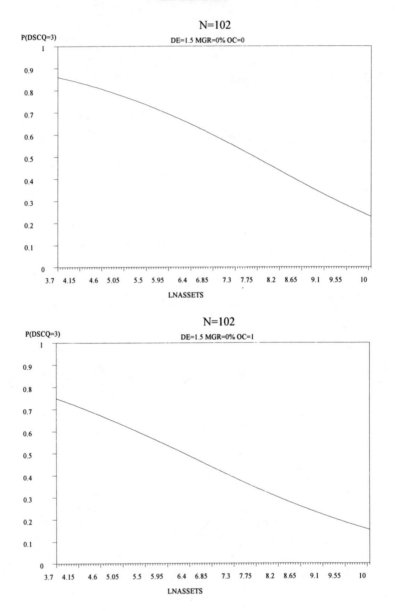

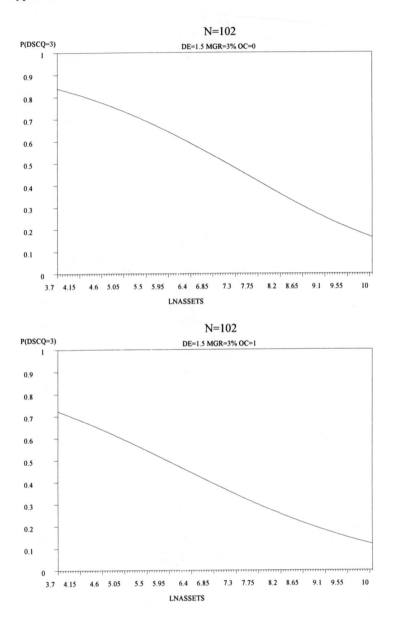

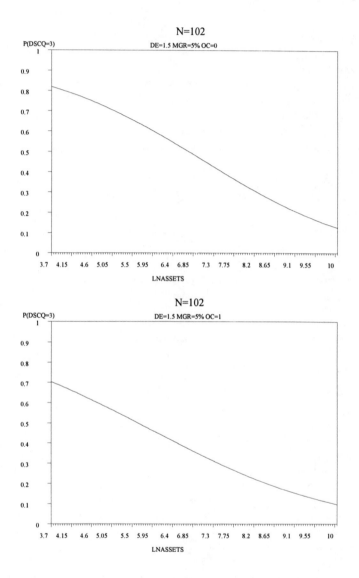

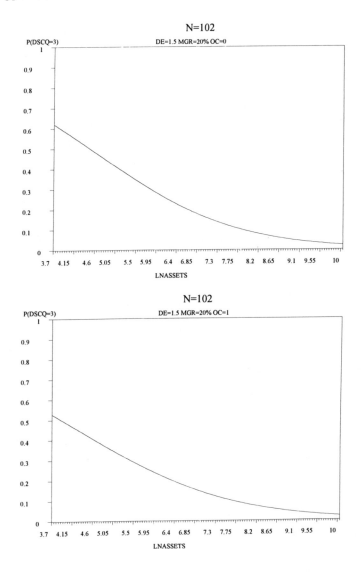

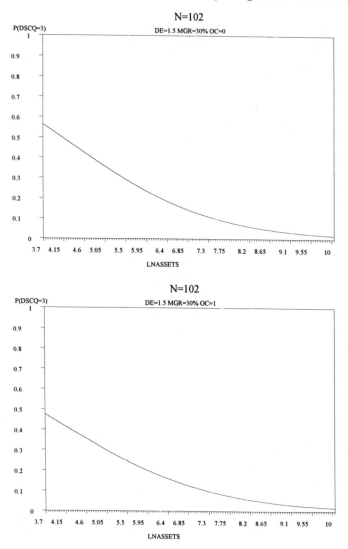

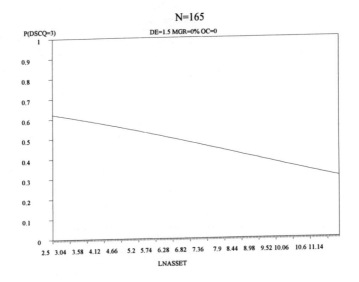

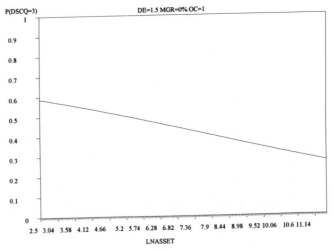

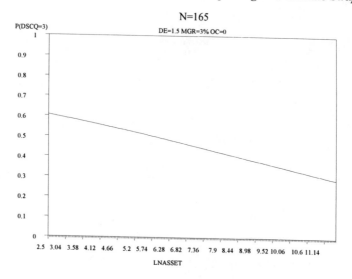

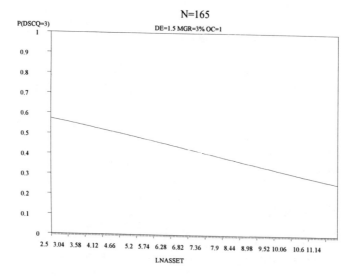

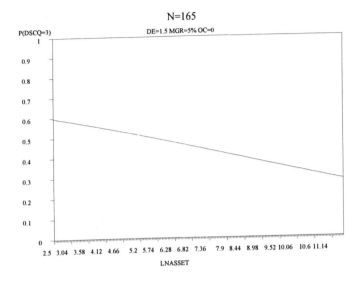

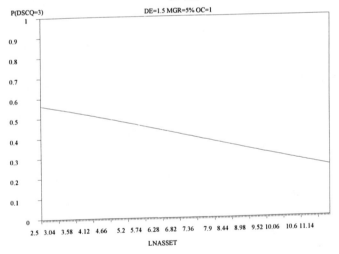

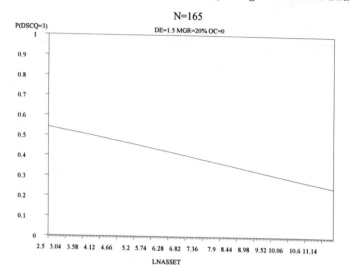

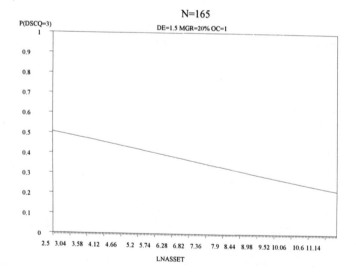

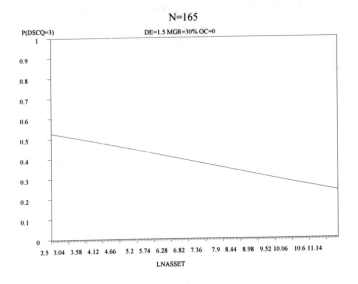

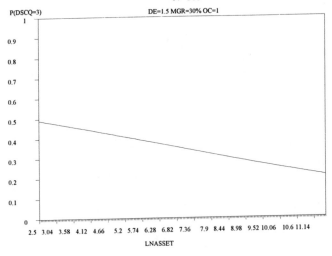

# CHANGES IN P(DSCQ=2 OR 3) OVER RANGES OF LNASSET

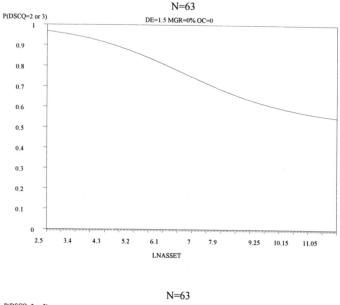

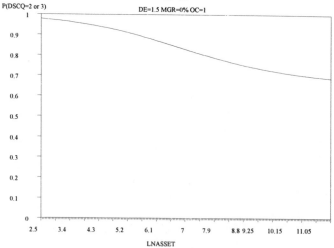

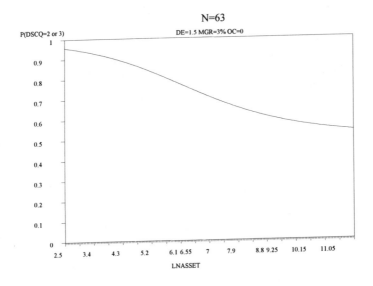

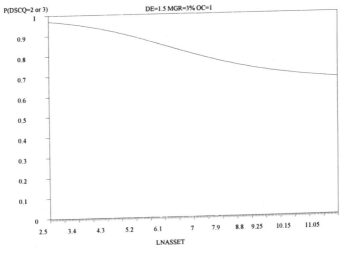

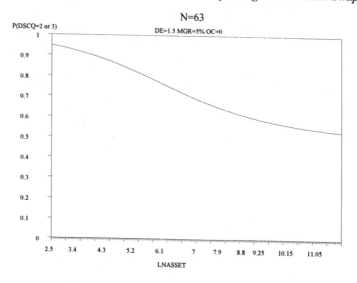

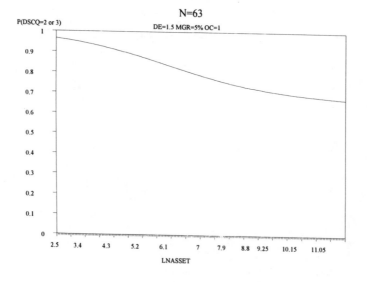

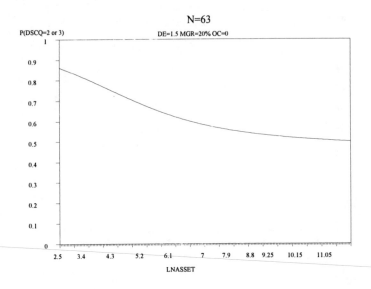

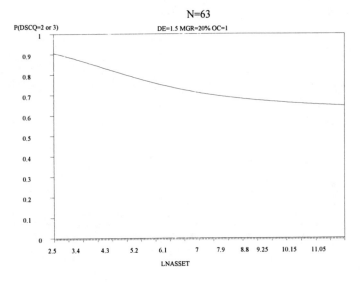

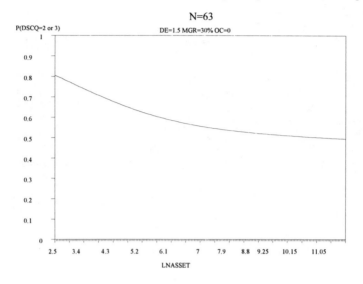

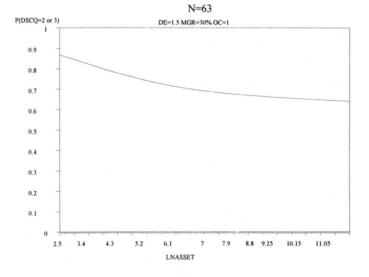

# References

Abdullah, Fuad A. and Virginia L. Bean. 1988. At Last, A Swaps Primer. *Financial Executive* 4 (July/August): 53-57.

Accounting Principles Board. 1972. *Opinion No. 26: Early Extinguishment of Debt.* (October) American Institute of Certified Public Accountants, Inc.

Alchian, Armen and Harold Demsetz. 1972. Production, Information Costs and Economic Organization. *The American Economic Review* 62 (December): 777-795.

Aldrich, John H. and Forrest D. Nelson. 1984. *Linear Probability, Logit, and Probit Models.* Beverly Hills and London: Sage Publications.

Altman, Edward I. 1968. Financial Ratios, Discriminant Analysis and the Prediction of Corporate Bankruptcy. *The Journal of Finance.* 23 (September): 589-609.

Altman, Edward I. Robert G. Haldeman and P. Narayanan. 1977. ZETA Analysis. *Journal of Banking and Finance.* 1:29-54.

Amemiya, Takeshi. 1981. Qualitative Response Models: A Survey. *Journal of Economic Literature.* 19(December): 1483-1536.

Anderson, James C. and David W. Gerbing. 1984. The Effect of Sampling Error on Convergence, Inproper Solutions, and Goodness-of-fit Indices for Maximum Likelihood Confirmatory Factor Analylis. *Psychometrika.* 49 (June):155-173.

Arak, Marcelle, Arturo Estrella, Laurie Goodman, and Andrew Silver. 1988. Interest Rate Swaps: An Alternative Explanation *Financial Management* 17 (Summer): 12-18.

Arnold, Tanya S. 1984. How To Do Interest Rate Swaps. *Harvard Business Review* 84 (September/October): 96-101.

Bagozzi, Richard P. and Youjae Yi. 1988. On the Evaluation of Structural Equation Models. *Journal of the Academy of Marketing Science.* 16 (Spring): 74-94.

Ball, Ray. 1990. What Do We Know About Market Efficiency? Paper presented at the American Accounting Association 1990 Doctoral Consortium.

Ball, Ray and Philip Brown. 1968. An Empirical Evaluation of Accounting Income Numbers. *Journal of Accounting Research* (Autumn): 159-178.

Barniv, Ran. 1990. Accounting Procedures, Market Data, Cash-Flow Figures, and Insolvency Classification: The Case of the Insurance Industry. *The Accounting Review.* 65 (July):578-604.

Bartlett, Sarah. 1986. They Swapped - and They're Sorry. *Business Week* 2948 (May 26): 111.

Beaver, William H. 1966. Financial Ratios as Predictors of Failure. *Journal of Accounting Research.* (Supplement): 71-111.

_____ 1981. *Financial Reporting: An Accounting Revolution* Prentice-Hall contemporary Topics in Accounting Series.

Beidleman, Carl R. 1985. *Financial Swaps* Dow Jones-Irwin.

Bentler, P. M. and Douglas G. Bonett. 1980. Significance Tests and Goodness of Fit in the Analysis of Covariance Structures. *Psychological Bulletin.* 88: 588-606.

Bentler, P. M. 1985. *Theory and Implementation of EQS, a Structural Equations Program.* Los Angeles: BMDP Statistical Software.

Bentler, P. M. and Chih-Ping Chou. 1987. Practical Issues in Structural Modeling. *Sociological Methods & Research.* 16:78-117.

Berle, A. A. Jr., and G. Means. 1932. *The Modern Corporation and Private Property.* Commercial Clearing House.

Berle, A. A. Jr. 1959. *Power Without Property.* Harcourt, Brace & Co.

Bicksler, James and Andrew H. Chen. 1986. An Economic Analysis of Interest Rate Swaps. *Journal of Finance* 41 (July): 645-655.

Bierman, Harold Jr. 1987. Accounting for Interest Rate Swaps. *Journal of Accounting, Auditing and Finance* 2 (Fall): 396-408.

Bowen, R. J. Lacey and Eric Noreen. 1981. Determinants of the decision by firms to capitalize interest costs. *Journal of Accounting and Economics.* (August): 151-179.

Brady, Simon. 1989. Hedging is Not Only For the Big Boys. *Euromoney* special supplement (October): 2-4,8,10.

Brealey, Richard and Stewart Myers. 1984. *Principles of Corporate Finance* New York: McGraw-Hill.

Brown, Keith C. and Donald J. Smith. 1988. Recent Innovations in Interest Rate Risk Management and the Reintermediation of Commercial Banking. *Financial Management* 17 (Winter): 45-58.

Bullen, Halsey G., Robert C. Wilkins and Clifford C. Woods. 1989. The Fundamental Financial Instruments Approach. *Journal of Accountancy* 168 (November): 71-73,75,77-78.

Burgstahler, David, James Jiambalvo and Eric Noreen. 1989. Changes in the Probability of Bankruptcy and Equity Value. *Journal of Accounting & Economics* 11 (July): 207-224.

Chow, Gregory C. 1960. Tests of Equality Between Sets of Coefficients in Two Linear Regressions. *Econometrica.* 28 (July):591-605.

Coase, Ronald. 1937. The Nature of the Firm. *Economica.* 4 (November). reprint, *The Firm, the Market, and the Law,* Chicago: University of Chicago Press. 33-55.

Cooper, Ian A. and Antonio S. Mello. 1991. The Default Risk of Swaps. *Journal of Finance.* 46 (June):597-620.

Cummings, Barbara K., Nicholas G. Apostolou, and William G. Mister. 1987. Accounting for Interest Rate Swaps: An Emerging Issue. *Accounting Horizons.* 1 (June):19-24.

Demsetz, Harold. 1983. The Structure of Ownership and the Theory of the Firm. *Journal of Law and Economics* (June): 375-390.

Dhaliwal, Dan S. 1980. The Effect of the Firm's Capital Structure on the Choice of Accounting Methods. *The Accounting Review.* 55 (January): 78-84.

Dhaliwal, Dan S. Gerald L. Salamon and E. Dan Smith. 1982. The Effect of Owner Versus Management Control on the Choice of Accounting Methods. *Journal of Accounting & Economics* 4: 41-53.

Dietrich, J. Richard and Robert S. Kaplan. 1982. Empirical Analysis of the Commercial Loan Classification Decision. *The Accounting Review.* 57 (January): 18-38.

Donaldson, Gordon. 1986. *Strategy for Financial Mobility* (2nd edition). Harvard Business School Press.

*The Economist.* 1990. Punters or Proprietors? (May 5).

_____. 1991. Survey: International Finance. 319 (April 27):5-46.

Eaker, Mark R. and Jess B. Yawitz. 1984. *Macroeconomics.* Englewood Cliffs, N.J.: Prentice-Hall.

Fama, E. 1980. Agency Problems and the Theory of the Firm. *Journal of Political Economy* (April): 288-307.

Fama, E. and M. C. Jensen. 1983a. Separation of Ownership and Control. *Journal of Law and Economics* (June): 301-326.

_____ 1983b. Agency Problems and Residual Claims. *Journal of Law and Economics* (June): 327-349.

FASB (Financial Accounting Standards Board). 1990. *Statement of Financial Accounting Standards No. 105.* Disclosure of Information about Financial Instruments with Off-Balance-Sheet Risk and Financial Instruments with Concentrations of Credit Risk. Financial Accounting Series No. 089. (March). Norwalk, Connecticut: Financial Accounting Standards Board.

_____ 1989. *Proposed Statement of Finanial Accounting Standards.* Disclosure of Information about Financial Instruments with Off-Balance-Sheet Risk and Financial Instruments with Concentrations of Credit Risk. Financial Accounting Series: No. 083-B. (July 21) Norwalk, Connecticut: Financial Accounting Standards Board.

_____ 1988. *EITF Abstracts.* A Summary of Proceedings of the FASB Emerging Issues Task Force. (October 6) Norwalk, Connecticut: Financial Accounting Standards Board.

_____ 1987. *Proposed Statement of Finanial Accounting Standards.* Disclosures about Financial Instruments. Financial Accounting Series: No. 054. (November 30) Stamford, Connecticut: Financial Accounting Standards Board.

_____ Description of FASB Project on Financial Instruments and Off-Balance-Sheet Financing, Staff Report (2164W).

_____ 1984. *Statement of Financial Accounting Standards No. 80* Accounting for Futures Contracts. (August) Stamford, Connecticut: Financial Accounting Standards Board.

_____ 1975. *Statement of Financial Accounting Standards No. 6* Classification of Short-Term Obligations Expected to be Refinanced. (May) Stamford, Connecticut:

Fornell, Claes. 1983. Issues in the Application of Covariance Structure Analysis: A Comment. *Journal of Consumer Research.* 9 (March): 443-448.

Fornell, Claes and David F. Larcker. 1981. Evaluating Structural Equation Models with Unobservable Variables and Measurement Error. *Journal of Marketing Research.* 18 (February): 39-50.

Forsyth, Randall W. 1985. The $150 Billion Baby: Interest Rate Swaps are Growing by Leaps and Bounds. 65 *Barron's* (August 19): 15, 36-39.

Foster, George. 1986. *Financial Statement Analysis* Englewood Cliffs, New Jersey: Prentice-Hall.

Francis, Jere R. and Earl R. Wilson. 1988. Auditor Changes: A Joint Test of Theories Relating to Agency Costs and Auditor Differentiation. *The Accounting Review* 63 (October): 663-682.

Hagerman, Robert. and Mark E. Zmijewski. 1979. Some Economic Determinants of Accounting Policy Choice. *Journal of Accounting and Economics.* (April): 141-161.

Heath, Loyd C. 1978. *Financial Reporting and the Evaluation of Solvency. New York:AICPA.*

Holthausen, Robert W. 1990. Accounting Method Choice: Opportunistic Behavior, Efficient contracting, and Information Perspectives. *Journal of Accounting and Economics* 12 (January): 207-218.

Hocevar, Dennis, Ali-Maher Khattab, and William B. Michael. 1987. Significance Testing and Efficiency in LISREL Measurement

Models. *Educational and Psychological Measurement.* 47:45-49.

International Swap Dealers Association. 1991. Confidential Market Survey: Total Interest Rate and Currency Swaps.

_____ 1987. *The ISDA Report.* 2 (July).

_____ 1986. *Code of Standard Wording, Assumptions, and Provisions for Swaps.* New York: International Swap Dealers Association, Inc.

Jarzombek, Susan M. 1989. What You Should Know About Accounting for Financial Instruments. *The Financial Manager* 2 (November/December): 46-50.

Jensen, Michael C. 1986. Agency Costs of Free Cash Flow, Corporate Finance, and Takeovers. *The American Economic Review.* 76: 323-329.

_____ 1989. Eclipse of the Public Corporation. *Harvard Business Review.* (September-October): 61-74.

Jensen, Michael C. and William H. Meckling. 1976. Theory of the Firm: Managerial Behavior, Agency Costs, and Ownership Structure. *Journal of Financial Economics* 3: 305-360.

Jensen, Michael C. and Clifford W. Smith, Jr. 1985. Stockholder, Manager, and Creditor Interests: Applications of Agency Theory. *Recent Advances in Corporate Finance.* Edward I. Altman and Marti G. Subrahmanyam, eds. Irwin: 93-130.

_____ 1984. The Theory of Corporate Finance: A Historical Overview. *The Modern Theory of Corporate Finance.* McGraw-Hill: 2-20.

Joreskog, Karl G. and Dag Sorbom. 1989. *LISREL 7 Users Reference Guide.* Mooresville, IN: Scientific Software, Inc.

_____ 1988. *PRELIS A Program for Multivariate Data Screening and Data Summarization*. Mooresville, IN: Scientific Software, Inc.

_____ 1986. *LISREL VI User's Guide*. Mooresville, IN: Scientific Software, Inc.

_____ 1979. *Advances in Factor Analysis and Structural Equation Models*. Cambridge, Mass.: Abt Books, Inc.

Kaplan, Robert S. and Gabriel Urwitz. 1979. Statistical Models of Bond Ratings: A Methodological Inquiry. *Journal of Business*. 52:231-261.

Kay, Robert S. 1985. The Financial Instruments Revolution. *Journal of Accounting, Auditing & Finance* 9 (Fall): 67-73.

Kerlinger, F. N. 1986. *Foundations of Behavioral Research*, 3d ed. New York: Holt, Rinehart and Winston.

Lau, Amy Hing-Ling. 1987. A Five-State Financial Distress Prediction Model. *Journal of Accounting Research*. 25 (Spring): 127-138.

Leftwich, Richard. 1983. Accounting Information in Private Markets: Evidence from Private Lending Agreements. *The Accounting Review* 58 (January): 23-42.

Lev, Baruch. 1989. On The Usefulness of Earnings and Earnings Research: Lessons and Directions From Two Decades of Empirical Research. *Journal of Accounting Research* 27 (Supplement): 153-192.

Lewis, Vivian. 1989. Stop and Swap. *Bankers Monthly* 106 (October): 82-4.

Light, Jay O. 1989. The Privatization of Equity. *Harvard Business Review*. (September-October): 62-63.

Loehlin, John C. 1987. *Latent Variable Models*. Hillsdale, New Jersey: Lawrence Erlbaum Associates, Inc.

Loeys, Jan G. 1985. Interest Rate Swaps: A New Tool for Managing Risk. *Business Review*. Federal Reserve Bank of Philadelphia. (May/June): 17-25.

Long, J. Scott. 1983. *Confirmatory Factor Analysis*. Beverly Hills and London: Sage Publications.

Maddala, G. S. 1983. *Limited-dependent and Qualitative Variables in Econometrics*. New York: Cambridge University Press.

Marais, M. Laurentius, Katherine Schipper and Abbie Smith. 1989. Wealth Effects of Going Private for Senior Securities. *Journal of Financial Economics* 23: 155-191.

Marais, M. Laurentius, James M. Patell, and Mark A. Wolfson. 1984. The Experimental Design of classification Models: An Application of Recursive Partitioning and Bootstrapping to Commercial Bank Loan Classifications. *Journal of Accounting Research*. 22 (Supplement): 87-114.

Marsh, Herbert W. 1985. The Structure of Masculinity/Femininity: An Application of Confirmatory Factor Analysis to Higher-Order Factor Structures and Factorial Invariance. *Multivariate Behavioral Research*. 20 (October): 427-449.

Marshall, John F., and Kenneth R. Kapner. 1990. *Understanding Swap Finance*. Cincinnati, Ohio.: South-Western.

McFadden, Daniel. 1974. Conditional Logit Analysis of Qualitative Choice Behavior. *Frontiers in Econometrics*, Paul Zarembka, ed. Academic Press. 105-142.

Mensah, Yaw M. 1984. An Examination of the Stationarity of Multivariate Bankruptcy Prediction Models: A Methodological Study. *Journal of Accounting Research*. 22 (Spring): 380-395.

Morck, Randall, Andrei Shleifer and Robert W. Vishny. 1988.
    Management Ownership and Market Valuation. *Journal of
    Financial Economics* 20: 293-315.

Muthen, Bengt. 1984. A General Structural Equation Model with
    Dichotomous, Ordered Categorical, and Continuous Latent
    Variable Indicators. *Psychometrika.* 49 (March): 115-132

Nair, R. D., Larry E. Rittenberg, and Jerry J. Weygandt. 1990.
    Accounting for Interest Rate Swaps. *Accounting Horizons* 4:
    20-30.

News Report. 1986. *Journal of Accountancy* 162:14.

Niehaus, Gregory R. 1989. Ownership Structure and Inventory Method
    Choice. *The Accounting Review* 64 (April): 269-284.

Ohlson, James A. 1980. Financial Ratios and the Probabilistic
    Prediction of Bankruptcy. *Journal of Accounting Research* 18
    (Spring): 109-131.

Ollard, William. 1984. The Thrifty Way to Expand. *Euromoney*
    (December): 98-105.

Olsson, Ulf. 1979. Maximum Likelihood Estimation of the Polychoric
    Correlation Coefficient. *Psychometrika.* 44:443-460.

Olsson, Ulf, Fritz Drasgow and Neil J. Dorans. 1982. The Polyserial
    Correlation Coefficient. *Psychometrika.* 47:337-347.

Organisation for Economic Co-operation and Development (OECD).
    1988. *New Financial Instruments; Disclosure and Accounting,*
    Selections from the proceedings of an OECD Symposium on
    New Financial Instruments. (May 31-June 1).

Popper, Andrew. 1984. Matchmakers Heat Up the Swap Market.
    *Business Week* 2867 (November 5): 56.

Ricards, Trevor S. 1984. Interest Rate Swaps Offer Flexible Financing,
    Lower Interest Costs. *Cash Flow* 5 (December): 37-39.

Riley, William B., and G. Stevenson Smith. 1987. Interest Rate Swaps: Disclosure and Recognition. *The CPA Journal* (January): 64-70.

Rue, Joseph C., David E. Tosh and William B. Francis. 1988. Accounting for Interest Rate Swaps. *Management Accounting* 70 (July): 43-49.

Schipper, Katherine. 1981. Discussion of 'Voluntary Corporate Disclosure: The Case of Interim Reporting.' *Journal of Accounting Research* 19 (Supplement): 85-88.

Shapiro, A. and S. Titman. 1985. An Integrated Approach to Corporate Risk Management. *Midland Corporate Finance Journal* 3: 41-56.

Shirreff, David. 1985. The Fearsome Growth of Swaps. *Euromoney* (October): 247-260.

Smith, Adam. 1776. *The Wealth of Nations*. Modern Library.

Smith, Clifford W., Charles W. Smithson, and Lee McDonald Wakeman. 1988. The Market for Interest Rate Swaps. *Financial Management* 17 (Winter): 34-44.

_____ 1986. The Evolving Market for Swaps. *Midland Corporate Finance Review* 20-32.

Smith, Donald J. 1988. Measuring the Gains From Arbitraging the Swap Market. *Financial Executive* 4 (March/April): 46-49.

Steinberg, Dan. 1988. *LOGIT: A Supplementary Module for SYSTAT and SYGRAPH*. Evanston, IL: SYSTAT, Inc.

Stewart, John E. 1989. The Challenges of Hedge Accounting. *Journal of Accountancy* 168 (November):48-50,52,54,56.

Stone, Mary, and John Rasp. 1991. Tradeoffs in the choice Between Logit and OLS for Accounting Choice Studies. *The Accounting Review*. 66 (January):170-187.

Turnbull, Stuart M. 1987. Swaps: A Zero Sum Game? *Financial Management* 16 (Spring): 15-21.

Toyoda, Toshihisa. 1974. Use of the Chow Test Under Heteroscedasticity. *Econometrica.* 42 (May):601-608.

Wall, Larry D. 1986. Interest Rate Swaps in an Agency Theoretic Model with Uncertain Interest Rates. Federal Reserve Bank of Atlanta Working Paper Series (July): No. 86-6.

_____ 1989. Interest Rate Swaps in an Agency Theoretic Model with Uncertain Interest Rates. *Journal of Banking and Finance* 13: 261-270.

Wall, Larry D. and John J. Pringle. 1989. Alternative Explanations of Interest Rate Swaps: Theoretical and Empirical Analysis. *Financial Management* 18 (Summer): 59-73.

Watts, Ross L. and Jerold L. Zimmerman. 1986. *Positive Accounting Theory* Englewood Cliffs, New Jersey: Prentice-Hall.

_____ 1978. Towards A Positive Theory of the Determination of Accounting Standards. *The Accounting Review* 53 (January): 112-134.

Wayne, Leslie. 1990. Many Companies in Pennsylvania Reject State's Takeover Protection. *The New York Times.* 20 July, A1.

Weberman, Ben. 1985. Keeping the Faith. *Forbes* 135 (May 20): 44.

_____. 1986. More Freedom, Fatter Profits. *Forbes* 138 (July 14): 35-6.

Whittaker, J. Gregg. 1987. Interest Rate Swaps: Risk and Regulation. *Economic Review.* Federal Reserve Bank of Kansas City (March): 3-13.

Williamson, Oliver E. 1967. A Dynamic Stochastic Theory of Managerial Behavior. Edited by A. Phillips and O. Williamson. *Prices: Issues in Theory, Practice and Public*

*Policy*. Philadelphia, Pa.: University of Pennsylvania Press; cited in Dhaliwal, Salamon and Smith (1982, 43).

Wishon, Keith, and Lorin S. Chevalier. 1985. Interest Rate Swaps - Your Rate or Mine? *Journal of Accountancy* 160 (September): 63-84.

Zavgren, Christine V. 1985. Assessing the Vulnerability to Failure of American Industrial Firms: A Logistic Analysis. *Journal of Business Finance & Accounting*. 12 (Spring): 19-45.

Ziebart, David Allen. 1983. *Modeling the Utilization of Accounting Data: An Empirical Study*. unpublished Ph.D. dissertation, Michigan State University.

Zmijewski, Mark E. and Robert Hagerman. 1981. An Income Strategy approach to the Positive Theory of Accounting Standard Setting/Choice. *Journal of Accounting & Economics* 3: 129-149.

# Index